WHO AM I?

Who are we?

The answer to this question is not easy. Man has always wondered about this question, and many different answers have been given. We can only think about some of these answers.

Some people say that man is just a mass of chemicals. This idea is called the "organic" view of man. This idea says that man is only flesh and blood, bone and muscle, but when this "stuff" dies, man is done. Not many people think this way. Most people believe that man is more than a chemical machine.

Another idea about man says that he is more than a machine. It says that man not only has a body, but that he also has a mind and a spirit. Man is different from other creatures. Other creatures do not wonder about themselves as man does. Other creatures just want to survive and be comfortable. But if the human mind is not sick or retarded, it wants to solve problems and find answers to questions which we will be asking in this book, and many more which we will not have time to ask.

However, it is more than man's mind which urges him on. When the spirit of man is touched by the power of God, man wants something more out of life than food, drink, shelter, and comfort. The spirit of man can remain selfish and afraid, or it can be turned to courage and goodness. A tiger is always a tiger, and a horse will always be a horse; but a human being, when touched by God's grace, rises far above any other creature which God has placed on earth.

The Bible tells us that when God made man He breathed into him "the breath of life; and man became a living soul" (Gen. 2:7). God did not make man as men would make a machine.

Now let us ask, "Is man good or evil?"

This brings us to what we will call a "point of reference." A point of reference is something against which we can compare ourselves. If we are going to find out whether we are good, we must have a point of reference, or something which we know is good.

For the Christian, the point of reference is God. The Bible teaches us that God is good. Jesus made this clear.

Because God is good, He is our point of reference. If we can know more about God, then it is possible for us to know more about that which is good. However, we cannot know about the goodness of God unless we can see that He is good, and this is one of the reasons why Jesus came to earth.

The Bible tells us that God came to man in the form of a man whose name is "Jesus." Therefore, our first source of knowledge is the Bible.

Without the Bible we could not know about Jesus, and without Jesus we could not know about God. If we do not know God, then we do not know what is good.

Now you can see why the Bible is our most important source of knowledge and why we must make the Bible the center of our studies.

The main question for us is, "What does the Bible teach us about man?"

The Book of Genesis (the first book of the Bible) tells us about the beginning of things. It tells us about God the Creator, and also about the man God created. Genesis gives us the first answer to the question, "Who are we, and what is man?"

In the very first sentence of Genesis we read,

"In the beginning God created the heaven and the earth."

Later in the same chapter we find these words:

"Then God said, 'Let Us make man in Our own image, after Our likeness, and let them have dominion over the fish of the sea, and over the birds of the air, and over the cattle, and over all the earth, and over every creeping thing that creeps upon the earth.' So God created man in His own image, in the image of God He created him; male and female He created them" (Genesis 1:26, 27).

What kind of creation had God made? Genesis tells us,

"And God saw everything that He had made, and, behold, it was very GOOD" (1:31).

The word "good" is used at the very beginning. What God made was good because God is good. This also means that man was made good. This also means that man was something like God, for he was made in the "image of God." In the beginning man was good and God's whole creation was good. Man was healthy and pure. If he stayed as he was, man would never die. Man had been created to live forever.

Among the gifts God gave man was the freedom to choose and decide many things for himself. This freedom to choose and decide is called the "freedom of the will." When man was created, he was given the freedom to obey God or to disobey Him. We shall see that man used his free will to disobey God.

Some people say that God should not have given man the freedom of his will because then man would not have disobeyed God. They say that if man had not disobeyed God everything would be much better for all of us now. Such persons think that man should not have had the power to "not love" God. But if one is not free to stop loving God, he is also not free to love God. Man can give glory to God only if he is free not to give glory to God. Only free people can love and glorify God. We shall see that man used his freedom to turn against God. When he did this, man also lost the freedom of his will. He could no longer love and glorify God. And this is man's biggest problem today.

When God created man, He made him in His own image; that is, man was perfectly holy, and he loved God with all his heart. Man was God's object to love, and God was to be man's object to love.

At the time of the creation God loved man, and man had the freedom to love God. Man did love God, and this mutual love for each other formed what is called a "communion." Man and God were in close communion with each other. This means that they understood each other. God understood man completely, and man knew many wonderful things about God. God and man were in fellowship with each other until something happened which changed this relationship of love.

God created man and gave him the whole earth. There wasn't a single thing man couldn't have except the fruit from one tree. He could have the fruit from the tree only if he decided to take it. But if he took it, he would take it against the will of God. Adam and Eve were happy and satisfied with all God had given them. Their happiness and joy was in God. Then something happened.

The Bible tells us that Satan, an angel who had turned against God, tempted man to wonder whether God was giving him enough. Satan tempted man to disobey God and eat the fruit which God told man not to eat. Man began to doubt God, and he also began to want more than God had given him.

Satan put questions such as these into man's mind: If man knew more, could he not be more like God? Or, could he not be another god? If this sounds strange, you need only think about yourself for a moment. Can you say that you have always been perfectly satisfied with what you are getting out of life? Aren't there times when you want more things than you have? Don't you also become discontented with life as it comes to you? Although you have been richly blessed, is it not true that you sometimes forget about what you have and are disturbed because you do not have more? This was also the case with Adam and Eve.

They had everything the earth had to offer; yet they wanted to be like God. God had specifically told Adam what he should do. In Gen. 2:15-17 we read:

> *"The Lord God took the man and put him in the garden of Eden to till it and keep it. And the Lord God commanded the man, saying, 'You may freely eat of every tree of the garden; but of the tree of the knowledge of good and evil you shall not eat, for in the day that you eat of it you shall die.' "*

In this situation Satan came with his question: "Did God say, 'You shall not eat of any tree of the garden'?"

> *"And the woman said to the serpent, 'We may eat of the fruit of the trees of the garden; but God said, You shall not eat of the fruit of the tree which is in the midst of the garden, neither shall you touch it, lest you die.' But the serpent said to the woman, 'You will not die. For God knows that when you eat of it your eyes will be opened, and you will be like God, knowing good and evil' "* *(Genesis 3:2-5).*

Do you see the point of the temptation? "Did God really say this? Are you sure that He said that? Of course He didn't say it." Finally the question comes, "Is God trying to hold something back from you? Isn't it true that God is afraid of you, and also afraid that you will become like Him?" Questions like these finally ended in man's breaking the commandment of God.

The Bible says that Adam and Eve ate of the fruit of the tree. Genesis goes on to tell us what happened after this. The moment man broke God's commandment his relationship with God was broken. The act of man said, "God, I do not trust You. I do not have faith in You. I think that You are holding something back from me."

When man doubted God and disobeyed Him, he fell into sin and the communion between man and God was broken. The word "sin" means that man rebelled against the One who had given him life. When man sinned, he fell away from God and lost his freedom to seek the goodness of God or even to want it.

Remember now what we said about man's freedom to love and give glory to God. Having disobeyed God, man was no longer free to love or give glory to God. He could not choose what is good. He was a slave to all that was evil and his will became enslaved to sin. His will was not free to love God.

There are many people who do not want to believe this. They want to believe that man did not fall that far away from God. They think that man can still choose that which is good. They do not want to believe that every person is born as a slave of Satan and that, like Satan, they can only hate God. But if we get mixed up about this, we will be mixed up about everything.

When Adam and Eve disobeyed God and fell into sin, another new thing was added to the sad lot of man. For the first time there was fear. Adam and Eve knew what it was to be afraid of each other, afraid of God, and afraid of other creatures. When man is without God, he is always afraid of something. But the worst thing that can happen to man is to be afraid of God. Adam and Eve were so afraid of God that they tried to hide from Him, but they couldn't.

We do not have to read more than the first few chapters in our Bible to know that what had been at peace and in harmony with God was now at war with Him. It didn't take long before one man killed another. In fact, the first son born to Adam and Eve turned out to be a murderer. He killed his brother Abel.

The whole creation was at war, and man soon discovered that sin results in death. Sin always brings death because sin is rebellion against God, and God is life. Man is still at war with God. He has not been able to change himself. This means that you are also at war with God. You want your own way. You are born with your will set against God, wanting only that which pleases you. You cannot change yourself from what you are. Only God can change you and make you want to do what pleases Him.

Perhaps some people wonder why Adam and Eve would be so afraid. They were afraid because they knew that they had something to fear — now they must die. God had warned them, "The day you eat of the fruit of the tree you shall surely die." Although God still loved Adam and Eve, His perfect justice and righteousness began to operate against their sin. Even though Adam and Eve must die, God immediately moved to restore them to life everlasting. God could not save their bodies from growing old and dying because the seed of death had been planted in them by sin. But God by His mercy could save them from sin, death, and the devil. And that He does save sinful man is the most wonderful truth in the Bible that we can know.

Because you are a sinner you are going to die. And if God does not fight the battle for you and win you away from Satan, you are doomed to live throughout all eternity as a rebel, separated from God. You will live forever in hell. The good news is that God has fought the battle and won it for you. The purpose of this book is to tell you this good news of a Savior so that you will want to live under God in His kingdom and serve Him.

We are now back to the first question we asked: "Who are we?" The answer is that we are descendants of Adam and Eve. It was not possible for Adam and Eve to have children who were not stained with sin and death. Because Adam and Eve had this defect, their children and their children's children would also suffer from the same disease of sin.

The goodness of man was gone. Man was helpless. He could not save himself. He had become evil by his very own act. He had rebelled against God. This is what the Bible teaches. Man no longer had original goodness. Now man was possessed by the disease of original sin.

"Original" means that the disease is in every person from the day he is born. Original sin is the opposite of original goodness. Our sins separate us from God unless we are restored once again to His presence. There is no way in which we can do this by ourselves. God must do this for us.

Now let us put the teaching of the Bible to a test. If man is born with sin, then certainly there must be some way for us to see that this is true. We will turn to the findings of some scientists to see what they have to say about man. First we must understand that science only describes what it sees in man, and it will use different words than those used in the Bible. However, what some scientists say about man is most interesting, and something all of us should know.

Science tries to describe what it sees in man. Let us begin by noticing how science looks at the newborn baby. Does science think that a baby is innocent, loving, and kind? Or, does science think that the baby is some kind of a vegetable? While there are those scientists who think that man is neither good nor evil, there are others who have noticed that the human baby is selfish and greedy.

Some scientists have noticed that there are selfish and destructive forces in the newborn baby, and that the human baby has two main concerns for itself. First, it wants to live (survive) and, secondly, it wants to be made comfortable. We should notice that these are the concerns of any animal, and in this sense a human baby is an animal.

If the human baby is left to itself and if it is never trained or changed, it will always be selfish, self-centered, and destructive. Selfishness and self-centeredness is the opposite of what God is. God is unselfish. God is love. God is good. Therefore we can say that a newborn child is not like God. In fact, the human baby is an opposite of God in many important ways. Science would call this being "unsocialized," which simply means that unless the child is changed he will not be able to live successfully with other people. The Bible, too, says that the child must be changed; it says that unless the child is "born again" or made new, it cannot live with God. Therefore God's first purpose for sinful man is to give him the opportunity to have a new birth in Christ. God wants man to get off to a new start so that he can live in communion with his Creator.

Who are we, and what are we like? We are sinners. We are, in our original form, hostile, selfish, unkind, and at war with God, with man, and even with ourselves. This is the disease from which we suffer and from which we must be saved if we are to have eternal life. We must be saved if we are to be in the kingdom of God, and if we are to have life with God. As we shall see, this cannot be done by ourselves. God must do this for us, and He does this through His grace. We cannot earn our salvation from the disease of sin and death. God must come to us as our Healer through Jesus Christ.

Now we will turn to the first article of our faith to find some answers to the question, "What is God like?"

what do I believe?

WHAT DO I BELIEVE?

There are three kinds of people in the world. First, there is the great majority of persons who believe in some kind of god. Secondly, there are those who don't know whether there is a god. Finally, there is a small group who do not believe in any kind of supreme being.

The Apostles' Creed is a statement about the God in whom Christians believe. However, first we should understand the different kinds of thoughts which people have about God. You should find this interesting and helpful.

THE ATHEIST. The atheist says that he does not believe there is a god.

The word atheist comes from the Greek word "theos," which means "god." By putting an "a" before "theos" you get the Greek word "atheos," which means "without God." But an atheist is also "against" God.

An atheist is a person who usually finds it necessary to argue and take a stand against God. An atheist is what we could call "an active unbeliever." Actually the atheist is at war against God. This is especially true in atheistic communism, where the leaders of the people have been working to eradicate the idea of God from the people's minds. Because of this, many Christians have been put to death by atheists in Russia and China. In many cases church buildings have been converted into factories and warehouses. The altars of the churches have been destroyed. But atheistic communism has failed to destroy the idea of God. Atheism fails because God is more than an idea in the minds of men. God is a person. God is eternal. He is the same yesterday, today, and forever.

In our country one doesn't hear too much from the atheist. Sometimes atheists find their way into the news by opposing released-time instruction in the public schools (but not all who oppose this are atheists). Or they will take a public stand against anything which might offend them, such as the motto "In God We Trust" which is placed on our money. The atheist will also assert that religion is superstition, foolishness, and a drug of the people. Most of the time you will find atheists presenting their ideas in classrooms of universities and colleges, or in certain political groups. Since you may come in contact with an atheist, it would be good for you to know something about his way of thinking.

The atheist usually needs to argue. He also counts on getting ahead of you in an argument. This he tries to do by asking certain questions which seem impossible to answer. For instance, he will ask, "How do you know that there is a god? Have you ever seen God?" Many Christians do not know that they can counter this question with another one. The atheist can be asked, "How do you know that there is no god? For this is what you are trying to prove."

Always remember that the atheist says, "There is no god," and if he can expect you to prove that there is a god, then he should also be prepared to prove that there is no god. Actually it does not pay to argue with an atheist, but sometimes it is necessary.

You should also understand that the atheist is in a very difficult position. His position is difficult because he cannot deny that he lives in a world which is filled with all sorts of awesome things. Like any other person, the atheist must wonder where all of these things came from. He must ask, "Where did the earth come from? What makes a blade of grass grow? Where did life come from, and how? What is life?" The Christian explains these things by saying that

God created the earth, the sun, moon, and stars, and that God gives life to every living thing. The person who does not believe in God must find some other explanation for these things.

The atheist says that everything happened by "accident." By this he means that there is no god, and that everything came into existence by luck or mistake. The atheist also says that there is no person or personality behind the world in which we live. We must examine this thinking further.

When you look at the world, you see many wonderful things. You know that the planets and other celestial bodies revolve in their orbits with more than clocklike precision. Astronomers can predict when an eclipse will take place many years from now. Man can figure out how far a star is from earth, or he can measure the speed of light, the speed of sound, and many other things. He can do this because the universe has a strange kind of order. You also count on this regularity when you do such a simple thing as setting your watch.

How did this amazing kind of order come about? Where did order and law come from? The atheist says, "It just happened by chance." Let us use an example to test this claim.

You will agree that a typewriter is a fairly complex piece of machinery. To be sure, it is not as complicated as many other machines, but it is something which most of us would not care to take apart and put together again. The typewriter was invented by someone who wanted to solve a problem. Several men had a hand in the improvement of the basic invention, which dates back to 1867. But before there could be a typewriter, there first had to be someone with a purpose and an idea. The problem was a better way to transmit thought to paper, and this was the purpose behind the invention. First came the problem and the purpose, then experiments and development. Ideas were put down on paper, and finally into materials.

Now let us suppose that you were to take a bushel of iron ore from the Mesabi range. Suppose also that you started to throw this iron ore up in the air over and over again. How long do you think you would have to throw it up in the air before it would come down as a typewriter, or even a piece of steel? The question sounds ridiculous, doesn't it? Even so, if there must be a mind and purpose behind the invention and construction of a typewriter, must there not also be mind and purpose behind the universe, which is far more complex than a typewriter? If a typewriter does not happen by chance, how can we stretch our imagination far enough to say that this universe could have just happened by accident? But this is the argument which the atheist wants us to believe. Which is easier to believe — chance or God?

In the First Article of our confession we say, "I believe in God." The atheist would say, "I don't believe in God. I believe in luck and chance. There is no purpose in anything."

THE AGNOSTIC. The word "agnosticism" comes from the Greek language also. It is the belief that there are many things about which a person cannot be certain. Most of all, he cannot be certain that there is a god.

An agnostic is a person who says, "I don't know whether there is a god," and "I don't know what god is like, if there is a god."

In a way many of us are agnostics because there are things which we have not settled in our minds. One of the purposes of confirmation class is to find answers which God has given us about Himself.

Some people believe that being an agnostic is a great sin and that God will punish anyone who allows doubts to come into his mind. There are people who are afraid to be honest and say, "I am not sure if there is a god." Often they are too afraid to ask questions. This is not a happy situation because a person cannot grow up to be a thoughtful and honest Christian unless he first asks questions.

Jesus wanted His disciples to ask questions. In fact, Jesus asked them many questions. He asked His disciples, "Who do you say that I am?" Again and again He would ask, "What do you think?" Jesus might have asked questions because He understood that people cannot learn unless they are asking questions, wondering, and also doubting that certain things are true. This you must do also if you are to grow up emotionally, mentally, and spiritually.

In your early years you believe just about everything you are told. You believe your parents, your teachers, and your friends. As a child you have many questions on your mind, such as, "What is rain? Where does rain come from? Who made the sun? Why does it get dark? What makes a flower grow? Where did I come from?" Perhaps at this time you are told about God, who made the world in which you live.

As you grow older you may begin to wonder about many of the things which you have been told. You might ask, "Is there really a god? I haven't seen Him. How do I know there is a god? Maybe there is no god. I don't really know what to think. Shall I believe everything I have been told?" When you say, "I don't really know what to think," then you have become an agnostic. This is not necessarily bad, depending upon what you do from then on. If you close your mind, as many people do, and think that you have nothing to learn, or that you are smart enough to have all of the answers, then you are on very dangerous ground. But if you are always searching for answers with the prayer that God will lead you to the truth, then you will find your search to be worth the effort you put into it.

Doubts can be very good for some people who are trying to grow up. We might even say that doubts are a necessary part of growing up. But when you have doubts about God or anything, do not attempt to hide them. Do not feel guilty about your doubts, for God understands how your mind and faith must grow. Coming to certainty and faith is a "process," and God, through His grace, will come to minister to anyone who is sincere in his desire to know the truth.

One year, in a confirmation class the pastor read the story of God creating the earth and man. The story came from Genesis, and the class listened attentively. When the pastor had finished, a young lad looked at him and asked, "But, pastor, you don't really expect us to swallow all of this, do you?" The pastor said that he did not expect them to swallow anything. This opened the door for a big discussion, and the pastor discovered that several members of the class seriously doubted that things had happened as the Book of Genesis says. Some also said that they didn't think that they believed in God. The pastor's answer to this was, "If you don't believe in God, you must have reasons." As it turned out, they had been studying scientific explanations about how the world might have come into existence. They thought that there was a real difference between what science says and what the Bible teaches. After several weeks of study and questions, plus some long discussion periods, the class came to see that there is no real difference between what science and the Bible teach. The only difference comes at the very beginning. The beginning question is, "But how did things get started?" The Bible says that God created them, and that God is still active as the Creator. Many thoughtful scientists will also agree. But science cannot say this. Science can only "notice" that things did get started. Science will form theories and say, "Perhaps things got started this way or that way." But until science can prove something, it will not make positive statements. Like any other system of thought, science must also do some guessing. The true scientist is a very humble man who admits that he doesn't know very much about a lot of things. Also science will not say that God did, or did not, get things started, because science has not proved either of these statements to be true or false. Therefore, if you hear someone say, "God didn't get things started," you can be sure that this is not a scientific statement.

It is good to say here that science is one of the most wonderful gifts which God has given man. Science is not the enemy of the Christian. Science is our friend. Science tells us many important things we should know. It tells us about the laws in our universe and the earth on which we live. It also tells us some things about ourselves which we need to know. While science cannot prove that there is or is not a god, it does point to the laws of the universe, and the scientist also must wonder where these laws come from. The Christian says that the universe and the laws have come from God. The agnostic will say, "As yet I do not know where the order comes from. Maybe it is God, but I don't know."

This brings us to the point where we should learn that there are two kinds of people who call themselves agnostics. There are true agnostics and false agnostics. The true agnostic will say, "I don't know, but someday perhaps I will find out." The false agnostic will say, "I don't know, and because I don't know, therefore it can't be true." True agnosticism can be good, but false agnosticism is nothing less than pride and utter stupidity.

We have considered two groups of people; that is, the atheist and the agnostic. Most people say that there is some higher power which they may call "God." We will look at three of these ideas about God.

1. PANTHEISM. Again we have a Greek word made up of two other words. First there is the word "pan," which means "all," and also the word "theos," which means "god." Putting them together, we have "pantheos," or "pantheism," which means that all is God.

According to the pantheist God is in everything. He is in the flowers, the trees, the birds, and the bees. He is also in all men. God is all of nature, and He is everywhere and in everything. Pantheists often use the word "nature" in place of saying "God."

To some people pantheism sounds good, but it is only good on the surface. The pantheist does not believe that God is a person. The pantheist believes that God is an impersonal "force," and a force without personality. Or, he believes that God is a "presence" in everything.

The pantheist does not believe that God has come to this earth as a person, but the Christian believes that He did come in the person of Jesus Christ, the Son of God. The pantheist tries to get himself "in tune" with nature (whatever this means), but he cannot offer prayers, because he does not believe that God is a person who can answer prayer.

2. DEISM. A second idea about God is called deism. The deist believes in God, or what he calls the "deity." He believes that God created everything, but also that God is no longer active in the world. God, for the deist, is somewhere outside of this world and not taking an active part in it. Therefore the deist cannot agree that God has entered into the world in the person of Jesus the Christ. The deist will say that God got things going but then withdrew Himself, and now the world is just rolling along without the presence of God in it. (We must say here that

all of these explanation are very simple and not completely accurate, but they are close enough to suit our purposes now.)

The deist sees no reason for asking God to answer prayer because God is "outside of the world." Just what the word "outside" means is not easy to say. The important thing is to notice that the deist says, "I believe in God," but this does not make him a Christian. The Christian believes that God is in the world, and that God is active in the world which He has made. The deist does not believe this.

3. THEISM. There are several kinds of theism.

Polytheists ("poly" means "many") are those who believe there are many gods. The ancient Greeks and Romans were such polytheists, as are many people in India and Africa today. Some of these believe in hundreds of gods.

Monotheists are theists who believe there is only one ("mono") god, a personal spirit who is concerned about the world which He made and is filled with love for that which He created.

The principal monotheists are the Jews, the Mohammedans, and the Christians. But the God of the Christians is different from the Jehovah of the Jews and the Allah of the Mohammedans in that He is one God, yet three Persons. This is the one true God as He is revealed in the Bible and as we confess Him in the Apostles' Creed.

The Apostles' Creed speaks about the three Persons in God. They are (a) God the Father, (b) God the Son, and (c) God the Holy Ghost (or the Holy Spirit). In other words, three different Persons are mentioned. This is where the word trinity comes in. Although our God is *"one God"* (cf. Deut. 6:4; 1 Tim. 2:5; Gal. 3:20), He has revealed Himself and still continues to show Himself to us as three different Persons. He has presented Himself to us as God the Creator, God the Redeemer, and God the Sanctifier.

As Christians we have been commanded to baptize all nations in the name of the Father, Son, and Holy Ghost. Therefore we say that even though our God is one God, He is also three Persons (Father, Son, and Holy Ghost), three in one, and one in three. (Cf. Matt. 3:13-17; 1 Cor. 1:3; 2 Cor. 1:2; Gal. 1:3; Eph. 1:2; Col. 1:2; Matt. 28:19.) But as you can see, words such as these are difficult to understand. That is why the Trinity is called a great mystery. We can see the Trinity at work, and we can experience it in many ways, but we cannot understand it. However, let it be known that even though the Christian confesses faith in Father, Son, and Holy Spirit, the Christian also confesses that He believes the Lord is One God.

Now let us turn to the word "creed." A creed is a statement of what one believes to be true. This brings us to the question, "What is God like, or what is the nature of God?" Although this is a poor question (because God is like Himself, and not like anything else), we ask it anyway.

Once when a pastor was taking a trip on a train, he met a young lawyer from Iran. The lawyer was a Moslem, which means that he did not believe in Jesus as the divine Son of God. The young Moslem lawyer and the pastor began to talk about their religions.

The Moslem told the pastor that a Moslem will never try to explain what God is like. He believed that no one should ever try to explain what God might be like. In fact he thought it an evil thing for a person to say, "God is like this and God is like that."

Moslems will only say what God is not like. For instance, they will say, "God is not evil," but they would not dare say that God is like Jesus. In other words, the Moslem only says what he thinks God is not, but he will not say what he thinks God is. At least this is what the young lawyer claimed.

Christians do not agree with this. Christians believe that they can know some things about God because God has given His children a picture of Himself. (We shall say more about this when we study the Second Article.) To be sure, we don't know everything about God, but there are some things of which we can be certain. This we believe. We believe because Jesus talked about God, and Jesus said,

> *"If you had known Me, you would have known My Father also; and from now on you know Him and have seen Him"* (John 14:7).

This simply means that when you look upon Jesus you are seeing some of the wonders of God in Him. As Jesus said,

> *"Believe Me that I am in the Father and the Father in Me" (John 14:11).*

Christians believe that Jesus is the picture of God the Father, and that He has been given to man so that man can see and know what God is like. When we have seen Jesus, we have seen the Father. But in order to see Jesus, we must turn to the Bible. Therefore, if we want to find out what God is like, we must open our Bibles and read about Him.

When we start saying what God is like, we are trying to describe Him. When we attempt to describe God, we begin to talk about His "attributes" as we have been able to see them in Jesus, in the Bible, and many other things. For instance, we can say that God is Love. Love is one of God's attributes, and this we will discuss later. Now let us list some of the attributes of God as they have come to us out of the pages of the Bible.

1. GOD IS ETERNAL. He has no beginning, and He will always be. As the psalmist said,

> *"Lord, Thou hast been our dwelling place in all generations. Before the mountains were brought forth or ever Thou hadst formed the earth and the world, even from everlasting to everlasting, Thou art God" (Psalm 90:1, 2).*

Of course, this is something we cannot begin to understand, simply because we are creatures who are tied down to time and space. We can't understand what the word "forever" means. So, when we say that God is eternal, it is impossible for us to imagine what this really means.

2. GOD IS UNCHANGEABLE. He says,

> *"I am the Lord, I change not" (Malachi 3:6).*

And of the Lord the psalmist says,

> *"Thou art the same, and Thy years shall have no end" (Psalm 102:27).*

It is important to know and believe that God does not change. While everything else comes and goes, and while nations rise and fall, God is the same yesterday, today, and forever.

3. GOD IS OMNIPOTENT. (God is almighty.) As Jesus said, "With God all things are possible" (Matt. 19:26). There is no might in the world like the perfect might of God. God is more mighty than all men and nations put together. Not even the forces of earthquake, flood, tornado, or hydrogen bomb can stand against Him.

With a word God made all things. With a word He can destroy all things. With a word He will bring forth a new heaven and a new earth. God is omnipotent. He is almighty.

4. GOD IS OMNISCIENT. (God knows all things.) Again the psalmist describes this attribute of God in beautiful words.

> "O Lord, Thou hast searched me and known me. Thou knowest my downsitting and mine uprising, Thou understandest my thought afar off. Thou compassest my path and my lying down and art acquainted with all my ways. For there is not a word in my tongue but lo, O Lord, Thou knowest it altogether" (Psalm 139:1-4).

And what a wonderful thing this is! God knows all there is to know about us. Nothing is secret to Him. No one will ever know us as God does. We can't even know ourselves as He knows us. And even though He knows who we are, and what we are like, God still loves us. This should make our hearts sing. Why should we fear to confess our sins to One who already knows all about us? Why should we attempt to hide from God when He knows all things? Nothing is kept secret from Him.

5. GOD IS OMNIPRESENT. (God is everywhere or anywhere as He pleases.) God says of Himself:

> "Am I a God at hand, saith the Lord, and not a God afar off? Can any hide himself in secret places that I shall not see him? saith the Lord. Do not I fill heaven and earth? saith the Lord" (Jeremiah 23:23, 24).

On the one hand we must say that God is everywhere, and in everything. This means that he is ruler over all things, and even has power over Satan himself. It also means that God is able to use both the good and the evil for His own purposes. But He is not everywhere because He has to be everywhere, nor does He have to make use of evil for His purposes. God still is the One who decides what He shall be doing. God is not limited. He can be anywhere and everywhere at all times. God is where He chooses to be, and if He chooses to be everywhere, this is His decision. He is not everywhere because we say He is. He is everywhere because He is God.

To the Christian this is a very wonderful truth. God is with us always. Jesus has promised to come to anyone who will not turn Him away. He says,

> *"Behold, I stand at the door and knock; if anyone hears My voice and opens the door, I will come in to him and eat with him, and he with Me" (Revelation 3:20).*

God is "Immanuel." This means that God is with us at all times. He is not far away from us. We do not have to wonder whether He will be with us. He is with us always. God is omnipresent. We cannot run away from Him. This is a most wonderful truth because even when we want to get away from God, He is still with us. Even when we rebel against Him, He is always there ready to forgive us. We praise God for this love.

6. GOD IS HOLY. (God is sinless, and He is pure.) God hates sin. He says, "I the Lord your God am holy" (Lev. 19:2).

It is impossible for us to imagine just what this means, because we are sinners. But we should try to understand something about the meaning of God's holiness. Perhaps we can use an illustration.

You all know that a person does not dare look at the blinding flash of an atom bomb explosion unless he wears very dark glasses. If one were to look at such an explosion at close range, he would be made blind by the terrible light. God's holiness is like this and even more so. God is so holy that man cannot look upon His holiness.

God had revealed Himself to the ancient Hebrew people as the holy God. God was so holy to them that they did not dare come to Him except under certain conditions. To emphasize His holiness, God permitted the people to approach Him in public worship only through certain specially chosen men called priests. They offered sacrifices to God for the people, who waited outside the sanctuary. Only one man, the high priest, was permitted to enter the Holy of Holies, the place where the Ark of the Covenant stood.

Somehow the holiness of God is being overlooked by many people, and we have forgotten that God hates sin with all the power of His being. We cannot come before God unless we have been cleansed of our sins. The forgiveness of sins is very important to all of us. We could not enter the kingdom of God and bring our sins with us, because God is holy. We should also understand that God does not think about sins as being little or big. God hates all sin. God is holy. God is without sin. He will not allow sin to enter into His kingdom. God will destroy all sin.

7. GOD IS RIGHTEOUS. (He does that which is right.) "For the ways of the Lord are right" (Hosea 14:9).

God is righteous and what He does is always right. When someone does wrong, he is unrighteous and therefore he must come under the judgment of the righteous God. Right and wrong do not go together. God demands righteousness, that is, unswerving obedience to Him.

Martin Luther knew this. He knew that God isn't just disgusted with sin, but that He hates sin. Luther knew that he was not righteous. He tried everything to become righteous so that God would not condemn him. But the more Luther tried to save himself from his sins, the more hopeless he became. How can a sinful man become righteous before God? This was the great question with which Luther struggled. He found the answer in God's Word. The righteousness which God demanded was not in man at all, but was to be found in Christ and His righteousness. These were the words of Scripture which brought peace to Luther: "For I am not ashamed of the Gospel of Christ; for it is the power of God unto salvation to everyone that believeth . . . for therein is the righteousness of God revealed from faith to faith; as it is written, The just shall live by faith" (Rom. 1:16, 17). God does not charge the sin of the person who believes in Christ against him! God covers the sin of the believer with the righteousness of Christ! The unrighteous man becomes righteous by faith. The believer takes hold of the perfect righteousness of Christ, and therefore he is not condemned by God. "Abraham believed God, and it was counted unto him for righteousness" (Rom. 4:3). "Therefore being justified by faith, we have peace with God through our Lord Jesus Christ" (Rom. 5:1).

This is the most wonderful truth of Scripture. We who are in Christ have the righteousness that satisfies the righteous God. By His free gift to us of His Son ("He hath made Him to be sin for us, who knew no sin; that we might be made the righteousness of God in Him," 2 Cor. 5:21), God, the righteous One, gives us that righteousness which we need to be His own and live under Him in His kingdom.

8. THE LORD IS GRACIOUS. The word "gracious" comes from the word "grace." This means that God gives us what we need even though we have done nothing at all to deserve His love and kindness. God moves toward us in grace. No man of himself has a right to anything from God. His gifts to us — rain, sunshine, food — are all free gifts of grace.

The most important gift of God's grace is the forgiveness of sins. We do not deserve this gift, because we are sinners. We cannot enter into the presence of God and ask anything at all, because we are sinners deserving nothing, absolutely nothing. But God is gracious. He does for us what we do not deserve, what we cannot do for ourselves. He gives us the gift of His Son Jesus Christ. He takes our sin on Himself and suffers the punishment which we really deserve. If God were not gracious, we would not have the forgiveness of sins. If God were not gracious, we would not be able to live with Him forever. God shows us kindness which we do not deserve. The Bible says:

> *"The Lord God, merciful and gracious, long-suffering, and abundant in goodness and truth, keeping mercy for thousands, forgiving iniquity and transgression and sin"* *(Exodus 34:6, 7).*

St. Paul says that God is gracious to save and has shown the exceeding riches of His grace in His kindness toward us through Christ Jesus.

> *"For by grace are ye saved through faith; and that not of yourselves; it is the gift of God; not of works, lest any man should boast" (Ephesians 2:8, 9).*

Because of all this we say that "we are saved by the grace of God." *Mark this carefully.* This means that there is no way in which we can save ourselves. We cannot earn or buy our salvation from sin, death, and the devil. God offers us salvation as a free gift of His grace. The Christian

trusts the merits of Jesus Christ counted to him for righteousness by a gracious God. This is the distinctive mark
of the Christian. His God is gracious.

9. GOD IS LOVE. The Bible shows that God is reaching
out to His children. As one reads the Book of Exodus,
one can see the actions of a loving God toward His people,
who were slaves in Egypt. We see how God brought them
out of slavery and finally into the Promised Land. We see
how He took care of His people.

But most of all, the picture of a loving God comes to us
through Jesus, and out of the New Testament writings.
Before Jesus came to earth, God's people knew that God
loved them, but they could not imagine what kind of love
this really was. Sometimes they thought that God would
give His love, and then that He would take it away from
them again. Jesus wanted all people to know that God
is Love.

When we say that God is Love, it is impossible to talk
about the meaning of this love unless we first say something about other kinds of love which are less than the
love God has for us.

In our English language we have but one word for love.
When we say "love," we can mean many different things.
First, there is the kind of love one "feels" when he meets
the girl of his dreams. Some of you are probably already
familiar with the strange feeling you get when you are
near a certain person of the opposite sex. Love at first
sight, it might have been. Something attracts you to another person. You don't know what it is, but you do know
that it is there. You lose your appetite and find it difficult
to concentrate on your schoolwork. Your parents see what
is going on, and perhaps they tell you that it is "puppy
love," or infatuation. This might make you furious because you are sure that this love is here to stay. But you
live to discover that "crushes" come and go.

This kind of love is called physical attraction. In our
language it is called love. But this is not the kind of love
that God is, nor is it the kind of love which God has
for you.

God is not infatuated with you. God is not fickle. Infatuation is fickle. It can be here today and gone tomorrow.

This is true of much so-called love seen in places such as Hollywood, where many people get married over and over again. As their infatuation with one another wears off, they "fall out of love" with one person and in love with another.

God's love is not on the human level at all. His love is totally unselfish and, unlike our human love, which is "bent in" on ourselves, it gives with no thought of return. If you give yourself to someone else, it is because that person is giving you something back. But God gives even though you are never able to return the same gift to Him.

We can talk about God's love, but it is impossible for us to imagine its full meaning. To think of someone who is able to give something to us with no thought of return, is difficult. God does just this.

God is Love. We do not say that God "was," or "will be," but we say that God "is" Love.

God is Love. This does not mean that some part of God is filled with love, but it means that God is totally Love. There is no part of God that is not self-giving love. 1 Cor. 13 is St. Paul's great description of this kind of love.

What then is love? Well, the first thing we can say about perfect love is that it is more than a power turned loose somewhere by someone. We often hear about the "power of love," but this is more than power. In its most perfect form, love is a person. That person is God. The highest kind of personality is that of total love. God is total Love. Love is expansive. It must keep moving and creating. Love is creative, and God is the Creator. Love always builds up that which is good. Although it has to punish evil and destroy it, love can never destroy just for the sake of tearing something down. If love tears something down, as God has torn down many nations, it is because this love is trying to build something else.

God's love is eternal. This means that His love will never die. Hate will die, but not love. Love cannot die, because God is Love.

Sometimes this is not easy to believe. There are people who would tempt us not to believe that God is Love. If we no longer believe that God is Love then we are also tempted to forsake the God who loves us.

The Bible tells us about the love of God. We see God's love in Jesus. Jesus is born in a stable for us. Jesus lived upon this earth for us. Jesus died on the cross for us. Jesus rose from the dead for us. Jesus, at the right hand of God the Father, is waiting for us. God is Love.

The love of God binds us to our Father in heaven. Read the words of St. Paul, who says,

> *"For I am persuaded, that neither death, nor life, nor angels, nor principalities, nor powers, nor things present, nor things to come, nor height, nor depth, nor any other creature, shall be able to separate us from the love of God, which is in Christ Jesus our Lord" (Romans 8:38, 39).*

We love God because He first loved us and gave Himself for us. The love of God must be given to other people through us. When people see us, they are to see the love of God shining through everything we say and do. Let us tell everyone that God is Love and that His love is eternal.

Let us now remember what we said about Jesus showing us what God is like. We said that we can know what God is like when we know what Jesus is like. Therefore, when we see that Jesus is Love, we know that God is Love. When Jesus gives up His life for us, it means that God has given Himself for us. When Jesus says, "Your sins are forgiven," we know that God forgives our sins.

God is Love. God is forgiving. God is good. Having said these things, we can now turn to the study of the Apostles' Creed.

who is God?

The illustration on the preceding page was chosen because it shows the Triune God, Father, Son, and Holy Spirit. In his print Dürer used the traditional method of representing God, the human figures for God the Father and God the Son, and the dove for the Holy Spirit.

THE APOSTLES' CREED

The First Article
Creation

I believe in God the Father Almighty, Maker of heaven and earth.

What does this mean? I believe that God has made me and all creatures; that He has given me my body and soul, eyes, ears, and all my members, my reason and all my senses, and still preserves them; also clothing and shoes, meat and drink, house and home, wife and children, fields, cattle, and all my goods; that He richly and daily provides me with all that I need to support this body and life; that He defends me against all danger and guards and protects me from all evil; and all this purely out of fatherly, divine goodness and mercy, without any merit or worthiness in me; for all which it is my duty to thank and praise, to serve and obey Him. This is most certainly true.

The Second Article
Redemption

And in Jesus Christ, His only Son, our Lord, who was conceived by the Holy Ghost, born of the Virgin Mary, suffered under Pontius Pilate, was crucified, dead, and buried; He descended into hell; the third day He rose again from the dead; He ascended into heaven and sitteth on the right hand of God the Father Almighty; from thence He shall come to judge the quick and the dead.

What does this mean? I believe that Jesus Christ, true God, begotten of the Father from eternity, and also true man, born of the Virgin Mary, is my Lord, who has redeemed me, a lost and condemned creature, purchased and won me from all sins, from death, and from the power of the devil; not with gold or silver but with His holy, precious blood and with His innocent suffering and death, that I may be His own and live under Him in His kingdom and serve Him in everlasting righteousness, innocence, and blessedness, even as He is risen from the dead, lives and reigns to all eternity.
This is most certainly true.

The Third Article
Sanctification

I believe in the Holy Ghost; the holy Christian Church, the communion of saints; the forgiveness of sins; the resurrection of the body; and the life everlasting. Amen.

What does this mean? I believe that I cannot by my own reason or strength believe in Jesus Christ, my Lord, or come to Him; but the Holy Ghost has called me by the Gospel, enlightened me with His gifts, sanctified and kept me in the true faith; even as He calls, gathers, enlightens, and sanctifies the whole Christian Church on earth and keeps it with Jesus Christ in the one true faith; in which Christian Church He daily and richly forgives all sins to me and all believers and will at the Last Day raise up me and all the dead and give unto me and all believers in Christ eternal life.
This is most certainly true.

WHO IS GOD?

The Apostles' Creed is not found in the Bible; it is a collection of teachings (from the Bible) which the first disciples taught. For this reason it is called the Apostles' Creed.

Luther's Catechism deals with the Apostles' Creed and other things which we shall consider. The Catechism is a collection of the teachings which are presented in the Bible. For this reason we will use the Catechism of Luther as a help to understand the meaning of these things.

THE FIRST ARTICLE OF THE APOSTLES' CREED

"I believe in God the Father Almighty, Maker of heaven and earth."

Notice that the creed begins with the personal pronoun "I." A creed is useless and meaningless unless someone is ready to say, "I believe." Until someone says this, the creed is dead. But this does not mean that the things about which the creed speaks are dead. God is not dead just because someone does not believe in Him.

"I believe." What does the word "believe" mean? This question is difficult.

We could say that it means, "I agree," or "I am sure that these things are true." But then we can also ask what it means, to agree or to be sure.

There are people who think that believing is something one has to feel. This could be right or wrong, or a little of each. St. Paul says, "With the heart man believes," and this seems to point to something which man will feel when he believes. But it is more likely that we are not sure just what Paul meant by this. We can be sure that he believed that there is something about believing which goes beyond the use of our minds. Believing is something more than agreeing that two and two are four. We can agree that two and two are four without stirring up too much excitement within us. But we cannot believe in God without having our personalities touched and changed in some way.

Perhaps Paul thought of the heart as being the center of our personality from which our personal powers arise. And one thing is certain — our personalities include our feelings. We must expect that believing in God will touch our feelings in some way, but we cannot be sure just how this is done, or just what it means.

This much we can say. When a person says, "I believe in God," there should be something more than just words. There should be some kind of action because he believes in God. These actions will be faith actions, for where there is faith in God a new power seems to be at work. People do things which they just wouldn't do otherwise. Jesus said, "By their fruits you shall know them." This means that a person with faith in God will be different from a person who does not believe in God.

Believers are different from nonbelievers. Believers are able to do what they could not do without faith and knowledge. Their personalities are changed for the better. There is something which makes it possible for them to do kind and loving acts. This thing which makes them live as Christians is faith in the things which they say they believe. When a person is an active Christian (and there is really no other kind), then his life says, "I believe."

The words "I believe" will be followed by some kind of action if the confession is sincere and true. If a person says that he believes in democracy, but never votes, we could doubt that he means what he has said. However, if he always votes but never says, "I believe," we still would know that he cares for his privileges and respects his democratic rights.

If a person says that he believes that all men are his brothers under God through Christ Jesus and then discriminates against any of his fellowmen, he denies what he has said; he does not believe his own words. If one calls himself a Christian, but lives an unchristian life, one can wonder what the words "I believe" really mean to him. If one believes in God, he will act accordingly. He will place his life in the hands of the God whom he confesses and has promised to serve. Placing one's life in the hands of God is an act of faith, and it is also the deepest meaning of the confession "I believe in God." This is something which cannot be done without the gift of faith. (See Articles Two and Three.) When an individual has been given the power to believe the many wonderful promises of God he rests secure in God's loving care, and does acts of faith.

> *"For it is God which worketh in you both to will and to do of His good pleasure" (Philippians 2:13).*

With this background we can now make the statement "I believe in God." We have some understanding of what it means to believe. We believe in a living God of love who cares for all that He has created.

Now we can go on to the next statement of importance. I believe in God "the Father Almighty, Maker of heaven and earth." This is our description of God as it comes to us from the Bible, and from the life of our Lord.

God is the Father, and God is the Creator. God made the heavens and the earth, and all living things. God is not limited. God can do anything except change Himself from what He is. God is Lord of all things.

The mightiness of God is easily seen in the Bible, for "with a word" God called all of creation into existence. With a word God will also bring all things to an end, and with a word God will establish a new heaven and a new earth.

God is almighty, and some of this mightiness has been given to man. With this might, man has done many wonderful things. He has built cities and nations, bridges and baseball fields, automobiles and aircraft. Man has also built bombs with terrible power for destruction, but in nothing has man approached the mightiness of God.

"Almighty" means "complete might." God holds all the power of the universe within Himself. All creative power belongs to Him, and also He has the power to destroy evil, which He shall do. There is nothing more powerful than God. He is the Maker of heaven and earth, as we confess in the First Article of the Apostles' Creed.

We now come to a most important question. The question is, "So what?" So what if God is the Father Almighty, Maker of heaven and earth?

In his explanation to the First Article, Martin Luther makes some important points which we want to consider, and he helps give us a good answer to "So what?"

Luther said:

A. "I believe that God has made me and all creatures." This is the answer to the question. You and I and all other people are creatures of God. God has made us, and not we ourselves. We are the products of God's creative power. We have come into existence because God is the giver of life. "God has created me." This is the first answer to "So what?"

B. The second answer could be, "that He has given me my body and soul, eyes, ears, and all my members, my reason and all my senses and still preserves them."

Without God the Creator, we wouldn't be. He has not only given us life, but He has also given us such things as are necessary to live in this life.

But what will a person do if he does not have some of these things about which Luther speaks? Let us suppose that a man suddenly loses his sight. What will he do?

There are several things he might do. He might accept his difficulties without too much of a struggle, or he might be angry with God for having allowed this to happen to him. But the Christian, even though he is lacking something, is one who is thanking God for what he has.

He is not being angry because he is lacking some other things. The Christian is one who understands that God has given him everything he has.

Now let us ask the question, "If God is so almighty and good, then why does He allow people to be born who are deaf, blind, or crippled?" Why are some people forced to go through life with a burden that is hard to bear? Doesn't this prove that God is not almighty, that God is not love, and that God is not present in the world? How can God allow so much physical pain and suffering if He is a God of love, and if He is almighty and able to stop suffering?

There is no easy answer to these questions. We just don't know why many of these things happen. However, we do know that there are many people who suffer these things, and still are able to believe that God loves them. It would be difficult for one to give an answer to these questions. We cannot say why a man is born blind. We might wonder about the problem as the disciples of Jesus did (John 9:2). When they saw a man who was blind, they wanted to know why he was blind, and they tried to find a reason. Jesus gave them the reason, but God does not give everyone a reason. The most amazing thing is that there are hundreds and thousands of blind people who can still say, "I believe in God the Father Almighty." They still believe that God loves them. The love of God shines through trials and tribulations, and the mightiness of God is still believed when His children are called upon to suffer. The history of the Christian Church tells many of these wonderful stories. One of them is about a man named Stephen.

Stephen was the first Christian to be put to death because of his faith in Jesus Christ. But before he died, he could pray for those who were stoning him to death. He prayed, "Lord, do not hold this sin against them" (Acts 7:60). The point of this is that Stephen's faith in an almighty and loving God still remained strong even when he was suffering terrible things. When Stephen died, his persecutors could not understand how he was able to smile. The answer is (Acts 7) that in his hour of death Stephen was able to see Jesus at the right hand of God. He saw the love of God in his hour of death. This is about all we can say in answer to many questions about suffering. We can say that even in times of suffering people have been able to see the love of God for them, and also the power and might of God. There are also many people who say that they probably would never have known the love and power of God except for their suffering.

While these are not answers for some people, they are answers which have been given by many who have suffered and are suffering. The only thing we can do is to cling to the truth given us in the Bible, that God is Love. While this does not give us an answer which we can understand entirely, at least it gives us an answer filled with power and might to work wonders in our lives. While God protected Luther from many dangers, God does not always prevent danger from coming to his children.

Speaking for himself and for Christians in general, Luther went on to say that "God has given and still preserves to me clothing and shoes, meat and drink, house and home, wife and children, fields, cattle, and all my goods; that He richly and daily provides me with all that I need to support this body and life."

But let us try to imagine what hungry Christians might think as they read these words of Luther. Of course we cannot actually imagine what such a person might be thinking. It wouldn't appear that such a person was being given enough to support his body and life, or that he was being defended against all danger, or protected from all evil. So where does the hungry Christian go for comfort and assurance that God is almighty, and that God loves him?

We cannot know the answer to these things unless we have been through the experience ourselves. But it is a fact that God's love has still been meaningful to people without bread or a place to live, and this is the important thing. If people know that there is an almighty God in heaven who loves them, even when they are hungry and cold, then there is something very powerful at work in their lives. If they can see fatherly divine goodness and mercy, in spite of their hunger and thirst, this seems to be extremely important and meaningful.

"I believe in God the Father Almighty, Maker of heaven and earth." We will read Luther's explanation to this article, and we may apply it to ourselves, if it fits. But let us understand that this explanation first belonged to Martin Luther. (His explanations to the Second and Third Articles apply to all Christians.) If what Luther describes fits you, then you have something which you can say about yourself while using his words. But if you are missing some of the things mentioned in Luther's words, then you will have to develop your own explanation as to what it means when you say, "I believe in God the Father Almighty, Maker of heaven and earth." The same holds true if you have blessings which Luther failed to mention.

For all of us it is finally necessary to make our own explanation to these words. The important question is, What do you mean when you say, "I believe in God the Father Almighty"?

Not everyone who says he believes in God is a Christian. A Christian is a special kind of believer. The Christian believes that God has come to live on earth in the form of a man. This "God-man" was Jesus. Jesus is the divine Son of God. Jesus is both true God and true man.

We have now said many things which will need further explanation. We shall attempt to explain some of these things, but we cannot explain all of them.

THE SECOND ARTICLE

1. "I believe in Jesus" is the first part of the Second Article. This means that we believe that there was such a person as Jesus, and that He really lived on the earth about two thousand years ago.

We know that Jesus lived, that He was born in Bethlehem of Judea, and that His mother's name was Mary. He grew up in Nazareth and worked in Joseph's carpenter shop. He preached in Judea, Galilee, and in Samaria. He was put to death in Jerusalem.

Most honest scholars will agree to these things. So when we say, "I believe in Jesus," the first thing we are saying is that we believe that He was a real person who once walked upon this earth among men.

2. I believe in "Jesus Christ." Now we add the name Christ. This increases the meaning of what we are saying.

Hundreds of years before Jesus was born there were people (the Children of Israel; the Hebrews) who were looking forward to the day when the Messiah (the Christ) would be born into the world. They believed that "the one who was to come" would make them a great nation once again. The Christ would lead them to victories over their enemies and give them their freedom.

The prophets (Isaiah, Jeremiah, Micah, etc.) had told about the "coming one." Therefore when we say that we believe Jesus is the Christ, we are agreeing that He is the one about whom the prophets were speaking or saying, "I believe that Jesus is the one who was to come as was foretold by the prophets of old," or, "I believe that Jesus is the Christ." It is interesting to note that the Hebrews are still waiting for the Christ to come. They do not believe that Jesus was the Christ.

There are two ways to use the name "Christ." You can say, "Jesus is the Christ," or you can say, "Jesus Christ." In the first case you say who Jesus is, and in the second case you use the name Christ as you would any other proper name.

3. I believe that Jesus is "His only Son." Jesus is God's only Son.

This is a very important part of our confession of faith. Every Christian will say that he believes that Jesus is the Son of God. But not everyone who says this always means the same thing. There are two important ideas about the meaning of the phrase "Son of God."

(A) "Son of God" means that Jesus did not have an earthly father as we do. The Bible tells us that the Holy Ghost worked a miracle in Mary and she gave birth to Jesus our Lord. Jesus was born of the Virgin Mary. The word "Virgin" (in this case) means that Mary was not married to Joseph when God made it possible for her to give birth to Jesus. Jesus had no earthly father. God is the Father of our Lord Jesus Christ, and Mary was His mother.

It is a waste of time to argue whether or not Jesus "could have" been born of a virgin. There are reports that it has happened, and these reports come to us from the Bible, and the Bible is our authority. The first meaning of "Son of God" is that God is the Father of Jesus. Joseph was the husband of Mary, but only the foster father, not the father of Jesus.

(B) "I believe that Jesus is the Son of God." In the second place this means that Jesus is "different" from all other men. God has an *only* Son, and He is Jesus. This point must be clear because there are people who like to say that all of us are "sons of God." The Bible says that we are sons of God, but the Bible still holds to the truth that Jesus is the "only" Son of God. How can we think about this?

Let us turn to the first chapter of the Gospel of John. There we read:

> *"In the beginning was the Word, and the Word was with God, and the Word was God" (John 1:1).*

Then, in verse 14, we see this astounding statement:

> *"And the Word was made flesh and dwelt among us."*

There it is. This "Word" is Jesus. Jesus was with God in the beginning. God in Jesus took on human form, was born of the Virgin Mary, walked here upon earth, and

> *"we beheld His glory, the glory as of the Only-begotten of the Father, full of grace and truth" (John 1:14).*

This is how Jesus is the Son of God. Jesus was with God in the beginning. Jesus was God in the beginning and Jesus was the Son of God as He walked among men. Jesus still is the Son of God. Jesus still is with God the Father, and Jesus still is God.

When we say these things about Jesus, it is not so difficult to see that even though we are "sons of God," there is much difference between ourselves and Jesus. We are "sons of God" because God has taken us unto Himself, but Jesus was with God the Father from all eternity. God has sent His *ONLY* Son to man. The only Son wants to bring others into the Kingdom of God. As people enter into the Kingdom of God, they are called "sons of God," and so we are.

If someone says to you, "I know that Jesus was a son of God, but so am I," you should understand that there is a difference between Jesus and any other human being.

Jesus is higher, more loving, gracious, kind, courageous, and holy than any other man, woman, or child ever to walk the face of the earth. No one can compare with Jesus. There has been no person who has been able to approach the glory of Jesus. Christians say, "I believe that He IS the Son of God, and that He is my Lord."

(4) I believe that Jesus is "true man," as Luther says in his explanation of the second article of the Apostles' Creed. Christians believe that Jesus Christ is (A) true God, and (B) true man. We want to talk about Jesus' being true man.

Jesus was born of a woman. He was born to live upon this earth. His first home was a stable because there was no room for Him in the inn. He had to be taken care of just like any other baby. He was a helpless child who had to be clothed and fed. His mother had to watch over Him, and Joseph had to take care of Him, too.

Jesus had to go to school. He wanted to learn the Bible, and when He was twelve years old He knew very much about the Holy Scriptures. He also had to work for His foster father in the carpenter shop. He was obedient to His mother and foster father. He had His tasks and chores to do like other children.

Jesus was true man. He needed to eat and sleep. He knew what it was to suffer sorrow and have deep joys. He also experienced the temptations of the devil. The devil was always ready to turn Jesus away from the thing He was supposed to do. The devil wanted Jesus to give up and not go to the cross. But Jesus won over temptation. He did not turn away from the thing He had to do for us. Although Jesus was born without sin, and even though He never sinned, He became sin for us when He went to the cross to die for us. Then He became the worst sinner that ever lived because the sins of all mankind were placed upon Him.

In so many important ways Jesus was just like us. But while Jesus was true man, He was also true God. Therefore Jesus was also different from us.

As we have said, Jesus had no sin. He was not a sinner until He took our sins upon Himself. When Jesus was born, He was like the first man God created, for Jesus and Adam were without sin. Adam disobeyed God and became a sinner. Jesus did not. Jesus was the kind of man God had intended Adam to be.

Because Jesus was truly the Son of God and also truly the Son of Man, Jesus was in perfect communion with His Father in heaven. The will of His Father was what Jesus wanted to do. He always prayed, "Thy will be done," and in this way He was very much different from us who are always trying to get our own way. Perhaps we could say that if we were without sin we would also be "true man." We are human beings, but we are not the kind of human beings God intended we should be. We are sinners, and we are born with rebellion in our hearts against God. Jesus was different. He was born without sin, and there was no rebellion against God in Him. Jesus was a true man as God wants all men to be. It would not be wrong to say that another meaning for the term "true man" is "sinless man."

(5) I believe that Jesus "suffered under Pontius Pilate." This fact is well known. It was Pontius Pilate, the Roman governor of Judea, who finally gave his consent that Jesus should die. The suffering of Jesus under Pontius Pilate was terrible. It was most terrible because Jesus could have escaped this suffering, but He chose not to do so. Jesus could have had help from heaven, but He stood up and listened to people accuse Him of many things of which He was not guilty. What is more, He was tried by a governor who was afraid of the people and afraid to go against their wishes. It was under Pilate that Jesus was beaten, mocked, spit upon, and crucified. This is the time in history when Jesus suffered, and Pontius Pilate was the Roman governor who permitted it to happen, even though he knew that Jesus was innocent. He was afraid to let Jesus go free.

(6) I believe that Jesus "was crucified, dead, and buried." Perhaps you know what crucifixion is, and maybe you don't. It was a most horrible way to put people to death. The one to be crucified was tied or nailed to a cross. Then he was left there to die. Death came because the body fluids were drawn off by the blazing sun. We cannot imagine the horror of such a death, and there is no real purpose in talking about it too much. But we should understand that crucifixion was a most cruel kind of death, and that it was

a common kind of execution in the days of Jesus. Jesus died on a cross, just like thousands of common criminals. But the death of Jesus was different from the thousands of similar deaths, and it was far more important. It was different and more important in the following ways:

First, Jesus went to the cross willingly. He knew that He must do it because this was the will of His Father. His Father wanted to have man restored in His Kingdom. This meant that man's sins had to be paid for and the punishment for his sins had to be suffered by someone. This punishment for sin and the guilt of sin was taken by Jesus for us. While He did this willingly, He also suffered terribly. He even prayed God that if it was possible for Him to escape He would want to escape. But there was no escape from the cross for Jesus, who loved us more than anyone will ever be able to love us.

Secondly, Jesus was not guilty of any crime against man or God. Others who were crucified were thieves and murderers. But not Jesus. He had done nothing wrong. He had committed no crime. Even Pontius Pilate had to say that he could find no fault in Jesus. This is another reason why His crucifixion was so different from other crucifixions. He had not been guilty of any crime.

Thirdly, Jesus was the most guilty man that ever walked the face of the earth in the sense that God made Him to be sin for us. Does this sound strange to you? First we say that He was guilty of no crime, and now we say that there was never a man more guilty than He. How can this be? Remember now how we have said that Jesus became sin for us. God made Him bear the guilt and punishment of every kind of sin that man has been able to commit. God punished Him for our sins of theft, murder, blasphemy, and every other kind of sin. All the sins of all men of all time were heaped on Him. All of the wrath of God against sin was flung at the cross, and Jesus bore it all for us. This is the real meaning of our Lord's suffering, and no one will ever suffer again as Jesus did for us. It is for you to remember always that He did this for you.

Jesus died on the cross on Good Friday. The entire earth was covered with darkness. Jesus had died within six hours. He died sooner than most men died from crucifixion.

It was not necessary for the soldiers to break His legs to hasten His death. Not a bone in His body was broken. And some of His friends went and asked Pilate whether they could take His body and bury it. He was buried in a rich man's tomb. He was dead.

(7) I believe that Jesus "descended into hell." Just what this means we do not know exactly. There is one reference to this in Scripture by the apostle Peter, who wrote that Jesus "went and preached unto the spirits in prison" (1 Peter 3:19), and from this the church has formulated the statement that Jesus "descended into hell." It is interesting to note that the Nicene Creed does not mention this.

The important meaning of Jesus' descent into hell is that He went to the center of Satan's world of evil to show Himself as being the victor over all evil, which certainly He is.

(8) I believe that on "the third day He rose again from the dead." This truth makes all the difference to us Christians, for

> "if Christ has not been raised, then . . . your faith is in vain" (1 Corinthians 15:14).

We must linger here, for it is the heart of our Christian faith, and it is exactly at this point where many people want to stop. Some people would say, "I can't imagine how such a thing could be, and therefore I cannot believe that it happened." However, there are many things happening in the world today which we cannot imagine, but we still believe in them. Most of us can't imagine what television is, and yet we believe that it is. We don't know what electricity is, and yet we use it. We can't explain what a grain of wheat is, and yet we eat bread. Therefore we would be slow of mind to use such a trick argument on ourselves. We would be wiser to turn to the Bible record. There was no doubt in the minds of the disciples that Jesus rose from the dead, and here is a most interesting story.

One thing is certain. The disciples of Jesus said that they had seen the Lord alive. They said that they had talked with Him, walked with Him, and that they had even touched Him. When the enemies of Jesus told them to stop telling this "nonsense" to other people, the disciples refused to be silent. "We must obey God rather than men," said Peter, and this they did. They were so sure of the fact that Jesus was risen from the dead that they could not be made to keep still. The result of their preaching brought much persecution, in which most of them gave up their lives for their Lord.

Jesus rose from the dead. His dead body was given life once again. The door of the tomb was flung open, and the tomb was empty on Easter morning when the women came to anoint the body of their Lord. He was not there. "He is risen," said the angel, and because He lives we also shall live. Just as He rose from the dead, we, too, shall rise to life eternal. We know now that death shall not be able to hold us, because it could not hold Him. There is eternal life waiting for us beyond the grave, and we shall worship God forever. Jesus said,

> *"Let not your hearts be troubled; you believe in God, believe also in Me. In My Father's house are many rooms. . . . I go to prepare a place for you . . . I will come again and will take you to Myself, that where I am you may be also" (John 14:1-3).*

This is why St. Paul could say,

> *"O death, where is thy sting? O grave, where is thy victory?" (1 Corinthians 15:55)*

This is why the early Christians could go to their deaths in the arena with faith, hope and courage. They knew that death was just the beginning of a wonderful new world which had been prepared for them by their Lord. For these, and many more reasons, it is important that we should know that on "the third day He rose again from the dead." Jesus says,

> *"I am He that liveth and was dead; and behold, I am alive forevermore. Amen. And [I] have the keys of hell and of death" (Revelation 1:18).*

(9) I believe that Jesus Christ "ascended into heaven." After Jesus rose from the dead He made many personal appearances to those who had known and loved Him. You can read about this in the Gospels.

It is interesting to see that none of Jesus' friends ever expected to see Him again. Even though Jesus had told them that He would conquer death, no one remembered what He had said. Therefore, when Jesus did rise from the dead, His resurrection took everyone by complete surprise.

After His resurrection from the dead, Jesus came to His friends (His disciples) and also to about five hundred other persons (cf. 1 Cor. 15:6). This is important, for it explains why His followers could be so sure that Jesus had risen from the dead. From this time forward the main message of hope was expressed in three words, "Jesus is risen."

After about six weeks Jesus called His disciples together and led them out of Jerusalem "as far as to Bethany" (Luke 24:50), where He "lifted up His hands and blessed them. And it came to pass while He blessed them, He was parted from them and carried up into heaven." (For discussion of heaven see the First Petition of the Lord's Prayer.) For our purposes we will say that Jesus returned once again to His former place with God the Father. Jesus came into the world of men, as a man. Now His visible presence was no longer with mankind. But Jesus is always present with His followers. He has said,

> *"I am with you always even unto the end of the world"*
> *(Matthew 28:20).*

At this very moment Jesus is with God the Father, but He is also with us. He said,

> *"Where two or three are gathered together in My name,*
> *there I am in the midst of them" (Matthew 18:20).*

While the visible presence of Jesus is no longer with man, this does not mean that Jesus is absent from the world. He is with those who believe in Him. He is present in the acts of worship which His children do. He is present in the Sacraments (see Sacraments). He is present where His Word is preached, taught, and obeyed. And He is present in His church (see Third Article). While Jesus has returned again to His former state of being with the Father, He is still present with those who believe in Him, and ready at all times to abide with anyone who will open the door for Him to come in to him. He says,

> *"Behold I stand at the door and knock; if any man hear*
> *My voice, and open the door, I will come in to him"*
> *(Revelation 3:20).*

(10) I believe that Jesus "sits at the right hand of God the Father Almighty." What this means we see from Eph. 1:20-23:

> *"He raised Him from the dead and set Him at His own right hand in the heavenly places, far above all principality, and power, and might, and dominion, and every name that is named, not only in this world, but also in that which is to come: and hath put all things under His feet, and gave Him to be the Head over all things to the church, which is His body, the fullness of Him that filleth all in all."*

Jesus has taken His former place, which He left when He came to live among men. Even now as true man He rules and governs the whole world for the good of His own people.

(11) I believe that Jesus shall come again to judge the quick (living) and the dead.

Jesus will come again. After Jesus "ascended into heaven" His disciples were told,

> *"You men of Galilee, why do you stand gazing up into heaven? This same Jesus, which is taken up from you into heaven, shall come again in a similar manner as you have seen Him go into heaven" (Acts 1:11).*

If His disciples could have recalled the words of Jesus, they would have remembered His saying,

> *"And they shall see the Son of Man [Jesus] coming in the clouds of heaven with power and great glory" (Matthew 24:30).*

One of the real questions has been, "When will Jesus come again to this earth?" Perhaps it would be good to look at this question because it has caused a great deal of confusion and strife in the Church. There are always those who are trying to tell when Jesus is coming again because Jesus talked about certain signs that would precede His coming. In fact, several times people have predicted the exact day and hour for the Christ's return to the earth. They have also quit their jobs and sold all of their possessions because they were convinced that Jesus was going to return on a certain day and at a certain hour. However, those who read their Bibles carefully will see that Jesus is not in agreement with this sort of thing. While the Bible tells that Jesus will certainly return, it does not tell when this return shall take place. Jesus says,

"But of that day and hour knoweth no man, no, not the angels of heaven, but My Father only" (Matthew 24:36).

So to summarize the teaching up to this point we can say: (a) Jesus will come again, (b) no man knows when He will come, (c) not even the angels in heaven know when He will come again, (d) only God knows the answer to this question.

The second coming of Jesus will be as a great surprise to everyone. The most surprised will be those who have not believed that He would return. But He will also surprise those who are waiting for Him to return, "for of the day, and the hour no man knows." He will come "as a thief in the night" (Matt. 24:42-44), or when He is least expected. While Jesus urged all men to be waiting, ready, and hoping for His return, He did not mean that His children should be afraid of His coming.

There are always people who want to frighten others by saying that the second coming of Jesus is something to be feared. While this is true for those who have rejected the grace of God, it is not true for the Christian. The Christian looks forward to the second coming of Jesus as His first disciples did, and as the church has done ever since those days. This is our great hope. The Christian prays that Jesus will come soon, for then a whole new world will be brought into existence, and there will be "a new heaven and a new earth" (Rev. 21:1). As John says,

"The first heaven and the first earth [shall then have] passed away. . . . God shall wipe away all tears from their eyes [from the eyes of His children]; and there shall be no more death, neither sorrow, nor crying, neither shall there be any more pain; for the former things are passed away" (Revelation 21:1-4).

The Christian looks forward to this hope. Jesus shall come again, and then wonderful things will take place. So we hope that Jesus will come soon.

However, there is also a reason for some to be afraid and filled with terror for we also confess . . .

(12) I believe that Jesus shall come again to *"judge the living and the dead."* In Matthew 25:31-46, Jesus talks

about this judgment. People shall be separated into two groups. Some will be given the everlasting kingdom of God, but the others will have to live forever without it. For those who cannot have the Kingdom, there will be much weeping and agony, for then these people will know that God is really God and that Jesus is Lord of all things. They shall have wasted their lives here upon earth. They will see that they have not allowed God to prepare them for the glory of His kingdom. Because they have thrown their lives away in squandering and waste, they cannot share the joys of the Kingdom. Jesus taught this in the parable of the talents. (See Matt. 25:14-30.) Only those who are prepared to receive the Kingdom can enter into it, as Jesus says in His parable of the ten virgins (Matt. 25: 1-13). Five were wise and had made proper preparations, while the foolish ones were overly anxious about other things, and not prepared to enter into the glory of their Lord.

There are many people who think that a loving God cannot allow people to live outside of His kingdom forever. But it is not God who does this to man. Although God makes the final judgment, it must be said that man chooses hell for himself. "How often I would have gathered you under My wing as a hen gathers her chicks, but you would not," said Jesus. And so the final judgment shall separate the wise from the foolish. The wise ones are those who have been "fools for Christ," as Paul has said. The wise are those who have not rejected the grace of God. They are the ones who believed that salvation comes from God alone, and not from man. They are the ones who seek first the kingdom of God, and therefore all other things are added unto them. It will not be so for the foolish, for they cannot understand or believe that they are lost. They think that they can save themselves without help from God or man. The cross of Jesus Christ is "foolishness and a stumbling block" to them. They cannot say that they are sinners who are in desperate need of God's grace. They are the proud. They receive the only possible reward for their own behavior. It is life without God.

Now let us turn to Martin Luther's explanation of the Second Article. Here are some of the most beautiful and meaningful words that have ever been written on this side of the Bible. Of all the parts of the Catechism, this portion should be held in memory to your dying day. Luther has this to say about the Second Article:

(A) "I believe that Jesus Christ, true God, begotten of the Father from eternity, and also true man, born of the Virgin Mary, is my Lord."

We have already discussed the fact of Jesus being true God and true man, and we also said something about Jesus being Lord. But hear Luther say, *Jesus Christ IS MY LORD!"*

The whole person and work of Jesus is summed up in the early Christian creed, "Jesus is Lord." St. Paul says that Christians will confess that Jesus is Lord.

> *"Therefore I want you to understand that no one speaking by the Spirit of God ever says 'Jesus be cursed!' and no one can say 'Jesus is Lord' except by the Holy Spirit"* *(1 Corinthians 12:3 RSV).*

"Lord" means ruler. He is the Ruler of our life and of all things. God has given Him a name above every name and placed Him above every other power. He is the Lord of the church and of the Christian's life. The Christian life does not exist apart from His lordship.

When one says, "I believe that Jesus Christ is *my* Lord," he places himself in faith under the lordship of Jesus Christ. The acceptance of His lordship is faith above all else. It means trusting the fact of liberation (Jesus my Lord has conquered the enemies of my life). It means trusting life to His commands (in faith I accept Him as Lord and become obedient to His will). It means living to serve Him. "He died for all that those who live might live no longer for themselves but for Him who for their sake died and was raised." (2 Cor. 5:15)

Many people want Jesus to save them from sin, death, and the devil, but they do not want Him to be their Lord. They don't want Jesus telling them what to do. They will not trust Him to take control of their life. Jesus once said, "Why do you call Me 'Lord, Lord,' and not do what I tell you?" (Luke 6:46 RSV).

When you in faith accept Jesus Christ as your Savior and Lord, you are ready to have Him take control of your

God the Redeemer

life. What will happen as you obey His will you have no way of knowing. What He will do with your life you do not know. But you trust Him as the Lord of your life. This is where faith comes in. Faith in His lordship means that you are ready to serve Him no matter what He wants to do with you. But regardless of what He does with you, He will always be with you. In love and faith you will disown any merit in yourself and will seek and pray for what Christ will give you. You can trust your life to His lordship. This leads right into Luther's claim for Jesus.

(B) I believe that Jesus "HAS REDEEMED ME, a lost and condemned creature, purchased and won me from all sins, from death, and from the power of the devil; not with gold or silver, but with His holy, precious blood, and with His innocent suffering and death." It would be possible for us to carry this statement on forever and ever. There is so much meaning in these words that one feels too small to think or talk about them, but we shall try.

Jesus Christ has redeemed me, a lost and condemned creature. First, there is the word "redeemed." It comes from the word "redeem." To redeem means to buy back, or to regain once again. In this case God has redeemed us from sin, death, and the power of the devil. As we saw in the introduction, man broke away from God, and became the captive of Satan. Now Jesus Christ redeems man and wins him for God. Man who is separated from God is placed in fellowship with God. Man who has lost his way is found by the love of God. Now we might wonder what it means to be lost.

When man is lost, he does not see things as they really are. So much is twisted and distorted for him, and he believes that everything (or many things) is more important than his life with God. While away from God, man is so concerned about what he shall eat, drink, and wear, that he cannot see God's vision for him. Lost man is selfish beyond the hope of saving himself, and he is filled with many destructive wishes. Lost man turns to false gods (see First Commandment) in the hope that he will find satisfaction and peace. However, the only thing he finds is fear, anxiety, and unhappiness. Worst of all, he thinks that he wants heaven, and he doesn't know that he is asking for hell. Lost man is confused, for although he has been created to love and serve God, he only serves and loves no one, not even himself. Lost man is loveless. While God has not taken His love from man, man has cut himself off from the love of God. Without the love of God, man, as we have seen, is a destructive creature. He enters into conflict, strife, and murder, even as Cain killed his own brother Abel. Lost man thinks that only by the use of force can he get what he needs, and he is also confused about what he really needs. He thinks that he needs "things" when he really needs God.

Finally, as St. Paul points out in Romans (chapter 1), lost man goes downhill into a destruction which makes him less human, and more like the animals who do not hesitate to fight and kill for what they want. Lost man is not "true man." Rather than being true man he is almost a true animal, but this he cannot see. His thinking and his desires are twisted in such a way that each step takes him farther away from God the Father, and this happens even when man thinks that he is making progress. The Bible tells this tragic story of man's downhill rush to destruction until he is far from God. There is no possibility for lost man to even see that he is lost, unless the Holy Spirit can touch him. Lost man is utterly incapable of redeeming himself. In no way can he buy his way back from the pit of hell into which he has sunk. The worst part of the tragedy is that man doesn't see how lost he is, or that he is lost at all. Rather than this, man goes on through life believing that he is the master of his own soul. He fails to see that he is a slave to his own foolishness, greed, and sin. He thinks that he is a free man, but he is a slave to sin, death, and the power of the devil. He is away from God, separated and lost. If man rejects the grace of God in Christ Jesus, he goes on to a final destruction from which he can never recover. It is from all of this, and much more, that God saves (redeems) man. And if man is not saved, then he is condemned. Luther said, "He has redeemed me, a lost and condemned creature."

You are acquainted with the word "condemned." A man commits murder and he is condemned to life in prison, or death. Even in our man-made laws (civil laws), we have punishment to fit the crime. So also in the realm of God's justice there is crime and punishment, and we must see that sin is not just a little mistake. Sin is crime against God. Every sin carries the death sentence with it. With God there are no big and little sins, or crimes.

We sinners are condemned to death because of our sin. It cannot be otherwise, for if God were to allow sin to enter into His kingdom, He would destroy Himself. God cannot allow sin to come into His kingdom, and every sinner is condemned to death. Every sinner includes all of us, and therefore all of us must die. We have been condemned to death because of our sin. And this brings us to the staggering good news of the Gospel without which we would have to despair.

St. Paul sums up the good news of the Gospel when he says,

> *"But God commendeth His love toward us, for while we were yet sinners, Christ died for us" (Romans 5:8).*

This is the same message as John 3:16: "God so loved the world that He gave His only-begotten Son that whoever believes on Him should not perish but have everlasting life." Do you see what this says? It says that even though we are condemned to eternal death without God, Jesus died in our place. Jesus took the full punishment for our sins. He "became sin" for us, and this sets us free from having to be without God. This saves us from a life and an eternity of hell. This brings us into the presence of God through the loving sacrifice of Jesus Christ for us. Yes, Jesus has redeemed us lost and condemned creatures.

"But," you may say, "we still must die." Yes, your body must die because your body is diseased by sin. But as we shall see, God will remake you one day and raise you from the dead, and take you unto Himself. You must remember that the death of your body is not because your sins are left unforgiven. Even though you are a forgiven sinner, your body is diseased, and it will die. However, Jesus says, "Because I live, you will live also." The resurrection of Jesus from the dead is our proof that we can really believe that we, too, shall live forever with God. When we have this hope, we are no longer lost. Our lives are pointed in a new direction. It is in God that the Christian lives, and moves, and has his being.

(C) Now we can attach the other words of Luther. How did Jesus redeem and buy you back from being a lost and condemned creature? Luther certainly presents the teaching of the Bible when he says that Jesus did not do this with any cheap kind of barter. He says, "not with gold or silver; but with His holy, precious blood, and with His innocent suffering and death."

What are we talking about here? Are we not talking about the Jesus who substituted Himself for us? Are we not speaking about the God who loved us so much that He gave His only-begotten Son to suffer the punishment for our sin and our guilt? Yes. Jesus is our Substitute who steps into this world to take the terrible wrath of the holy God upon Himself when we should be suffering that wrath ourselves.

Jesus was stricken, smitten, and afflicted by God because He became sin for us. Always remember this. Christ hangs on a cross and dies. His death is for you. His suffering is for you. His pain is pain you should have known. His separation from God is the separation which should be yours throughout all eternity. But He has redeemed you, a lost and condemned creature. He has done this with His holy, precious blood and His innocent suffering and death. Certainly you cannot understand such love as this, and you cannot understand the ways of God, who does all this for you. But this is how God gives you eternal life. This is how He brings you to heaven. This is how He has redeemed you.

Your hope for eternal life is to trust in God. Have faith only in God. This means that you are to trust what God has done for you. You are to trust His Word and His promises. You are to believe that Jesus has paid the full penalty for your sins. When you believe this, you are made just and righteous before God because the righteousness of Jesus Christ becomes your righteousness. You can enter into the presence of God confessing your sins without fear, and you can give Him honor and praise. You are no longer a stranger to God because Jesus Christ has removed the barrier which separated you from God. Your salvation from sin, death, and the devil depends only upon God's grace. When you believe that what Jesus has done is done for you, then you are justified by faith. Believe on the Lord Jesus Christ and you shall be saved.

As Christians we have faith in Jesus as our Substitute, and we believe that He has paid the full penalty for our sins. We trust only in Jesus Christ as the One who is able to save us from sin, death, and the devil. We do not trust ourselves or other people. We trust only Jesus. What is more, we do not trust what we are able to do. We will never be able to work our way into heaven. We can never be good enough to be in the kingdom of God because of the good things we are able to do. Only Christ Jesus can take us to heaven. Only our Substitute can save us. We are justified before God (we become right before God) through our faith that Jesus has done all things well and that He alone is our Savior.

(D) Finally, there is a purpose for everything, and there is also a purpose for our having been redeemed. Again Luther uses words which are filled with meaning. The reason for Jesus' coming to save us is "that I may be His own and live under Him in His kingdom and serve Him in everlasting righteousness, innocence, and blessedness." This is most certainly true. We have been saved to serve God. We can live under Him forever. This is the answer to the question, "Where do we belong?" and no other words are necessary. We belong with God. "For all which it is my duty to thank and praise, to serve and obey Him."

THE THIRD ARTICLE

I. "I believe in the Holy Ghost." (Spirit, Comforter.)

As we are in the process of growing up, we must grow in four different ways if we are to become more mature persons.

First, we must grow physically. This is the most natural kind of growth, for if we feed our bodies and take care of them, we will grow to physical maturity, provided that there is not something wrong with our health.

Second, there is mental growth. This is not so fast as our physical growth, and it is also less natural. If we want to grow mentally, then we must work to do so. We must develop our minds and our reasoning powers which God has given us.

Third, there is emotional growth. This means the ways in which we behave and react to people and situations, and even the way that we react toward ourselves. How we solve various problems depends in large measure upon our emotional maturity. Some people never stop behaving like little children, and they miss so much that life has to offer. But with some good guidance, and with some personal effort, one can also come to emotional maturity.

Finally, there is spiritual growth. This is the subject matter of the Third Article. This kind of growth, as we shall see, is not natural for us. While we can do something about the other kinds of growth, we can do nothing about this until the Holy Ghost touches our lives. The Third Article of the Apostles' Creed takes five points into consideration, and they are (1) the Holy Ghost (Spirit); (2) the holy Christian Church, the communion of saints; (3) the forgiveness of sins; (4) the resurrection of the body; and (5) the life everlasting.

The Holy Ghost is the third person of the Godhead. God the Father, God the Son, and God the Holy Ghost are three in one, and one in three.

Before Jesus left this earth He told His disciples that He would send "the Comforter . . . even the Spirit," to them (John 14:16, 17). He said, "I will not leave you desolate [without hope]; I will come to you" (John 14:18). The Holy Spirit would bring Jesus' disciples to a remembrance of all that He had said and done (John 14:26). The Holy Spirit would give them faith and courage to preach the Gospel to all nations, even in the face of persecution and death.

Let us now ask what the Holy Spirit does, and what work is accomplished by the Spirit. For these answers we can turn to the words of Martin Luther.

(1) "The Holy Ghost calls me," says Luther. There is much meaning in this word "call." Luther understands that man is by nature sinful and far away from God. He also knows that unless something happens, man will continue to live away from God. Even more than this, Luther understood that there was no way for man to find his own way back to God. If man was to return to God, he must be brought back to God.

The Holy Ghost (Spirit) calls us. We are called by the Gospel, which is the good news. God is seeking to bring all men into His kingdom, where they shall be granted forgiveness of sins, life everlasting, and the privilege to serve Him in everlasting righteousness, innocence, and blessedness. This gives us the picture of our God reaching out for man, who is lost and condemned and without Jesus Christ. God reaches out and calls us with His love. It is only in the Christian religion where one gets a picture such as this. Through His love for man, God calls,

"Come unto Me, all of you who are weary and heavy laden, and I will give you rest" (Matthew 11:28).

Again, God says,

"Though your sins be as scarlet, they shall be as white as snow" (Isaiah 1:18).

It is the Holy Spirit who calls us through the Gospel, and tells us that God loves us, that God seeks for us, that God wants us, and that nothing shall separate us from the love of God which is in Christ Jesus our Lord (Rom. 8:38, 39). Paul said, "He called you by our Gospel" (2 Thess. 2:14). Again:

"[God] hath saved us and called us with an holy calling, not according to our works, but according to His own purpose and grace, which was given us in Christ Jesus before the world began" (2 Timothy 1:9).

Notice how Paul stresses the point that this call has come to us not because we deserve it, not because we earned it, but because God loves us. We might also turn to the Revelation of St. John where he writes,

"The Spirit and the bride say, Come. And let him that heareth say, Come. And let him that is athirst come. And whosoever will, let him take the water of life FREELY" (Revelation 22:17).

Jesus also tells about the invitations, or calling, in His parable about the invitation to the great supper (cf. Luke 14:16, 17), and in the parable of the invitation to the marriage of the king's son (cf. Matt. 22:1-10).

(2) The Holy Ghost (Spirit) also "enlightens me with His gifts." Not only is lost man dead in his trespasses and sins, but he is also blind and ignorant. He does not know that there is a better life for him. He stretches himself to gain wealth, power, popularity, and physical security, but he can't see that he should "seek first the kingdom

of God" (Matt. 6:33). And while man may learn many wonderful things in science, philosophy, psychology, etc., he cannot be truly wise or enlightened until he has learned something more than this. In order to be made complete, man must know about God's love for him, and man must be captured by this love. But man cannot know these things by himself. Man is blind when it comes to these matters. If man is going to be enlightened, he must receive the new light from God. He said, "I am the Light of the world: he who follows Me will not walk in darkness, but will have the light of life" (John 8:12). And since it is the Holy Spirit who leads us to Christ, it is the Holy Spirit who brings us into the light.

It is possible for us to think our way out of a lot of ignorance, but we cannot think our way into the light of God's grace. We must be brought there by the power of the Holy Spirit, who calls, gathers, and enlightens us. Even the things about which Jesus spoke, and the things He did, do not make sense unless we are given the power to see what they mean. The Holy Spirit shows us the deeper meaning of life. That deeper meaning is in God's grace through our Lord Jesus Christ. Therefore we can say again that it is God's wonderful grace which saves us, for it is God's grace that empowers us to have faith, and we must have faith if we are to live in His kingdom and serve Him.

Let us turn to some passages in Scripture which can help us remember this important thought.

> *"You are a chosen generation, a royal priesthood, a holy nation, a peculiar people, that you should show forth the praises of Him who has called you out of darkness into His marvelous light" (1 Peter 2:9).*

Notice closely where the emphasis is . . . (God) "has called you out of darkness into His marvelous light."

> *"It is the God who said, 'Let light shine out of darkness,' who has shone in our hearts to give the light of the knowledge of the glory of God in the face of Christ" (2 Corinthians 4:6).*

Again, we see that God does the work of love in us.

It is important to know that we are enlightened through the power of the Holy Spirit. But it would not be good for us to bend so far over backward that we pay no attention to such things as science and the use of our own minds. Our minds, the tools of science, and many other things are also gifts of God's grace. We are in duty bound to make full use of that which our heavenly Father has granted unto us. Christians will want to know as much as they can. They will work to develop their minds and all of the gifts which God has given them. For us to sit idly by, thinking that we have no responsibility to seek more light, would not be in agreement with the words of Jesus Christ,

"Ask and it shall be given unto you, seek and ye shall find; knock and it shall be opened unto you" (Matthew 7:7).

(3) The Holy Ghost has "sanctified me in the true faith." This simply means that the Holy Ghost gives us the power to *reject sin* and to do that which is well pleasing in the sight of God. And "This is the will of God, even your sanctification" (1 Thess. 4:3).

When we are in the process of being sanctified, we are becoming new kinds of people. "If any man be in Christ, he is a new creature" (2 Cor. 5:17).

Our prayer should be that of David, who said, "Create in me a clean heart, O God, and renew a right spirit within me" (Ps. 51:10). Furthermore we should always understand that,

"We are His workmanship, created in Christ Jesus unto good works, which God hath before ordained that we should walk in them" (Ephesians 2:10).

The Holy Ghost gives us the power to grow to greater Christian maturity. He does this by assuring us that our sins are forgiven, and that God accepts us and loves us. He works with us so that we are more ready to serve God rather than man. He separates us from much which we once thought was so important. He transforms our selfish desires into more God-pleasing desires. This goes on day after day, moment by moment, experience by experience. As we face new problems, the Holy Spirit is ready and eager to give us the grace to make the Christian decisions which we should be making. This is a process which we call sanctification. It is the process of growing more Christlike day by day through the power and grace bestowed upon us by the Holy Spirit.

(4) Finally, what the Holy Spirit does for you and for me He also does for all believers. In like manner "He calls, gathers, enlightens, and sanctifies the whole Christian Church on earth, and keeps it with Jesus Christ in the one true faith [faith in Jesus Christ as Savior and Lord]; in which Christian Church He daily and richly forgives all sins to me and all believers, and will at the last day raise up me and all the dead, and give unto me and all believers in Christ eternal life. This is most certainly true." (Martin Luther)

What we have said is of great importance. As you can already see, the Christian religion has no place for man to say, "I am a believer because I decided to be a believer." Nor can man say, "I have faith in Christ because I thought good thoughts, and did good deeds." Faith in Jesus Christ comes from God as a free gift "which we do not merit," and which we cannot earn. This again is the meaning of grace. WE ARE SAVED BY GRACE THROUGH FAITH. God's grace provides us with the faith to believe in Jesus Christ and the power to be more Christlike.

We must stop here long enough to get this very clear in our minds. The difference between Christianity and other religions (at least one great difference) is that Christianity says that all things come from God. This includes food, clothing, shelter, and life itself. But it also includes faith, power, and finally salvation, which is brought to completion in the gift of eternal life. Whereas other religions teach that man earns his salvation, in Christianity, man is *given* salvation. This gift is a gift of *GRACE*. Therefore we say that we are saved by grace through faith.

There is something very important about this. In Christianity there is no room for pride. Every man, woman, and child is on the same level. They all have the same need. They all suffer from the same disease of original sin. They all have the same problem of not being able to save themselves. They all have the same hope that God, through the grace of the Lord Jesus Christ, will provide the solution to the problem of their salvation. Who then can boast and say, "This I have done"? No man can boast except in the Lord, says St. Paul.

It is the Holy Ghost who provides us with that kernel of faith which may be no larger than a mustard seed, but with this little bit of faith we can start growing as Christians. And this, then, is the meaning of sanctification. Sanctification is the process of growing to be more Christlike persons. Through His grace God gives us faith to believe in Jesus Christ, and also a desire to follow Him. We can take up our cross and follow Him only if we have faith that His promises are true, important, and eternal. We can attempt to do what He wants only if we are certain that what He is making of us is right and good. This requires faith, which we receive from God through the Holy Spirit. Faith is a gift of God to us.

Our God-given faith helps us take hold of the promised forgiveness, and helps us live more like Jesus has asked us to live. The more we live like Jesus, the more sanctified we become. The more we are sanctified, the more we follow in the footsteps of Jesus. Of all the different kinds of growth, spiritual growth is the most important. A person who is growing spiritually is also becoming emotionally mature and more human. He is becoming more like true man, as man was originally created and meant to be. And all of this is because of the work of the Holy Spirit. As Paul says, "May the God of hope fill you with all joy and peace in believing, so that by the power of the Holy Spirit you may abound in hope" (Rom. 15:13).

The Holy Spirit gives us new life in God and makes us Christians. As Luther says, "I believe that I *CANNOT* by my own reason or strength believe in Jesus Christ, my Lord, or come to Him; but the Holy Ghost *has called me by the Gospel, enlightened me with His gifts, sanctified and kept me* in the true faith." This also tells us that we remain Christians, and are kept in faith, through the power of the Holy Spirit. We do not come to faith in Jesus because of anything we do, and we are not kept in the faith by anything that we can do *of ourselves*. The Holy Spirit gives us faith in Christ as Savior and Lord, and the Holy Spirit keeps us in this faith unto life everlasting. Again, we have nothing about which we can boast except that we should boast in the Lord, and give all the glory to Him for the miracles taking place in our lives.

II. I believe in "the holy Christian Church."

This brings us to the consideration of the holy Christian Church. The first question we must ask is, "What is the holy Christian Church?"

When we first think of the "church," we often think about a building. Someone asks us, "Where are you going today?" We might answer, "I am going over to the church." You are using "church" to mean a building. You are not wrong in doing this because we have come to speak of churches in this way. "Church," to us, means the building in which we gather to worship God. But when we use the word church this way, we are not using it the way in which it was originally meant to be used, because the first Christians had no church buildings. However, there is nothing wrong when we call our place of worship a church.

In order to understand the meaning of the term, we must go back to the days of Jesus, for our Lord spoke about His church. Let us try to find out what He meant. One day Jesus said to Simon Peter, "Thou art Peter, and upon this rock I will build My church; and the gates of hell shall not prevail against it" (Matt. 16:18). Just before this, Jesus had asked some important questions. Jesus had questioned His disciples (see Matt. 16:13 ff.) by asking, "Who do men say that the Son of Man [Jesus] is?" Or, "Who do men say that I am?" The disciples answered, "Some say John the Baptist, others say Elijah, and others Jeremiah, or one of the prophets." Then Jesus asked, "But who do you say that I am?" Simon Peter replied, "You are the Christ, the Son of the living God." And Jesus answered him, "Blessed are you, Simon Bar-Jona! For flesh and blood has not revealed this to you, but My Father who is in heaven." In other words, Jesus is telling Peter that he knows something which he (Peter) could not have known by himself, but that this knowledge and faith had been given to him by God. It was a gift of grace.

Jesus then goes on to say, "And I tell you, you are Peter, and on this rock I will build My church, and the powers of death shall not prevail against it."

Now what did Jesus mean by this when He spoke about His church? It is certain that He was not talking about a building. But from this point on, there is an argument which we must consider. There are two ideas about what Jesus meant when He said, "Upon this rock I will build My church."

All of you know something about the Roman Catholic Church. The Roman Church believes that Jesus was saying that He builds His church on Peter. The Lutheran Church, and other Protestant churches, hold that this is not so. The Lutheran Church teaches that Jesus would build His church on faith such as Peter had when He confessed, "Thou art the Christ, the Son of the living God." We do know, that where there is no faith in Jesus Christ as the Son of God, there is no church. The church begins when a person simply says, "I believe that Jesus Christ is the only Son of God." This is the "rock" of the church. Without this rock of faith in Christ, there can be no church, even though there are large organizations with many buildings which are called the church. Faith comes through God's grace. Grace is given to us through His Word and Sacraments (see Sacraments), and therefore we can say with Luther that the church is present where the Word is preached and the Sacraments are administered. This (Faith, Word, Sacraments) is the rock of the church.

We are now brought back to the first point. The church is more than a building, and more than a man-made organization. However, Christians are most often organized into what we have come to know as "churches, congregations, or gatherings." These organizations elect officers, have constitutions, and conduct business. Sometimes the "organized church" is called the "visible church," or that which one can see. Then we also speak about the "invisible church," or that which we cannot see. The invisible church means the God-given faith which people have in Jesus Christ. It is this which binds people together in unity.

What shall we do with these ideas about the visible and the invisible church, and what shall we finally say that the church is? Martin Luther did not like to say "holy Christian Church" because he felt that it was confusing. He said that the church is nothing else than a congregation, or assembly of Christians (not necessarily organized). . . . "The church is the assembly of the pious, believing men of earth which has been called, gathered together, is ruled, and preserved by the Holy Ghost, and is daily increased by the means of the Sacraments and the preaching of God's Word."

What Luther is saying is that there is something "visible" about the church. But what is visible about the church is not necessarily the organization which people have put together. It is more than this. It is the "gathering" of people who have been brought together by the power of the Holy Spirit, and their common faith that Jesus Christ is the Son of God. And as they have been brought together by the Holy Ghost, they also partake of the Sacraments (Baptism and the Lord's Supper), and they preach, teach, hear, learn, and live the Word of God. Jesus has said, "Where two or three are gathered together *IN MY NAME,* there I am in the midst of them." So we could say that where Jesus is (in the midst of even two or three people), there the church is also. This gathering of people need not be in a special building, nor need it be organized as our congregations are organized today. This does not mean that we should do away with our church buildings and organizations, but it does mean that we should always understand that man cannot make, nor can man hold the church of Jesus Christ together by building organizations. The church of Jesus Christ is given life by the Holy Spirit, and held in union with Jesus Christ, through the power of the Spirit in the Word and the Sacraments.

Let us also remember we cannot live as Christians without other Christians, and therefore groups of some kind are necessary. There is no such thing as an "individual Christian." Christians need one another. They need to share the faith in Jesus Christ with one another. St. Paul talks about this when he is writing to the Christians in Rome. He had never seen them, but planned to visit them, and these are the words he used:

> *"For I long to see you, that I may impart to you some spiritual gift to strengthen you, that is, that we may be mutually encouraged by each other's faith, both yours and mine" (Romans 1:11, 12).*

One would think that if any Christian could have lived without the help of others, it would have been such a person as the apostle Paul. Paul gave his life for the sake of Jesus Christ and the Gospel. But the deeper one goes into his Christian faith, the more he understands that he has the need to give and receive, and that he needs other Christians with whom he can be. Paul had this need to share his faith in Christ with others, and to have others share their faith with him. He understood that he could not grow into spiritual maturity all by himself. He had a need to give and take. This is why it is foolish for a person to suppose that he can live as a Christian while keeping himself away from the congregation of believers. We must share with one another, or we find our faith dying. But this sharing must not only be the sharing of one another, it must be the sharing of the wonderful Gospel. The Holy Spirit keeps us in unity with each other, and with the Lord of the church.

The church is more than a building, and more than an organization put together by man. It is the gathering of people who believe in Jesus Christ. Most of all, the church rests securely on the only foundation, which is Jesus Christ, our Lord.

Paul says, "As we have many members in one body . . . so we, being many, are one body *IN CHRIST.*" The cement of the church is Jesus Christ. But Jesus is more than cement. Jesus is the life of the church. As you will remember, Jesus once told a beautiful story to His disciples. They were walking through a vineyard together. He pointed to a grapevine. From this vine came many branches. On the branches were leaves and fruit. Then Jesus said,

> *"Abide in Me, and I in you. As the branch cannot bear fruit by itself, unless it abides in the vine, neither can you, unless you abide in Me. I am the Vine, you are the branches. He who abides in Me, and I in him, he it is that bears much fruit, for apart from Me you can do nothing" (John 15:4, 5).*

Apart from Jesus Christ there can be no life, no church, no power. He is the life, and this life is given to us and to the church through the power of the Holy Spirit. The branches cannot give themselves life. The branches must take life from the vine, which is Jesus Christ. The branches are united through the vine.

Let us also remember that Jesus has said, "I will build My church." Therefore the words of Paul mean so much when he writes,

> *"So then you are no longer strangers and sojourners, but you are fellow citizens with the saints and members of the household of God, built upon the foundation of the apostles and prophets, Christ Jesus HIMSELF being the chief cornerstone, in whom the whole structure is joined together and grows into a holy temple in the Lord; in whom you also are built into it for a dwelling place of God in the Spirit" (Ephesians 2:19-22).*

Paul speaks of us as having been "built into the church."
We do not build ourselves into it. God builds us into the
church. The whole structure is JOINED TOGETHER,
AND GROWS INTO A HOLY TEMPLE IN THE
LORD. Upon the cornerstone which is Jesus Christ, the
church is joined together by the Holy Spirit, and the church
grows into a holy temple through the power of the Holy
Spirit. Therefore, let us now confess that the church is
God's doing, and not ours. We cannot form the church,
we cannot build the church, we cannot unite the church.
Neither can we or anyone else ever destroy the church
of Jesus Christ. Belonging to the church is belonging to
God. God cannot be destroyed.

*NO ONE OR NOTHING SHALL EVER DESTROY
THE CHURCH OF JESUS CHRIST.* This is important
for us to know, for there are some people who say that
one day there shall be no church. They think that time
will take care of the church, and that sometime in the
future the church will pass into history and be forgotten.
But remember the words of Jesus to His disciples when
He was talking about His church, "And the gates of hell
shall not prevail against it (My church)." This means
that one day the church shall overcome hell itself.

Every church building and every organization could be
destroyed, but the church of Jesus Christ will live on forever even through all eternity. The gathering of His people
shall always be here upon earth, and ever after in heaven.
This is something that guided missiles and hydrogen bombs
cannot destroy. No amount of persecution or hardship
has ever been able to wipe the church from the face of
the earth. Nothing will be able to do this now or in the
future. As Luther said, "Take they then our life, goods,
fame, child, or wife. . . . THEY YET HAVE NOTHING
WON, the Kingdom ours remaineth." And these are the
certainties of St. Paul, who writes,

> *"WHO shall separate us from the love of Christ? Shall
> tribulation, or distress, or persecution, or famine, or naked-
> ness, or peril, or sword? . . . No, in all these things we are
> more than conquerors THROUGH HIM WHO LOVED
> US. For I am sure that neither death, nor life, nor angels,
> nor principalities, nor things present, nor things to come,
> nor powers, nor height, nor depth, nor anything else in all
> creation, will be able to separate us from the love of God
> in Christ Jesus our Lord" (Romans 8:35-39).*

IF NOTHING CAN SEPARATE US FROM THE LOVE OF GOD WHICH IS IN CHRIST JESUS OUR LORD, then we, the believers in Jesus Christ, shall always be the church. This brings us to the answer we have been seeking. What is the church? The answer is, WE ARE THE CHURCH. We who believe in Jesus Christ as the Son of God — we who put our trust and confidence in Him — we who take hold of His promises that the Kingdom comes — WE ARE THE CHURCH. We are the gathering of the "saints." We who have been cleansed from our sins through the suffering and death of our Lord — we who have been born anew to a living hope through the resurrection of Jesus Christ from the dead, and to an inheritance which is imperishable, undefiled, and unfading, kept in heaven for you (1 Peter 1:3, 4) — WE ARE THE CHURCH OF JESUS CHRIST. We have been called, gathered, enlightened, and sanctified by the Holy Spirit through the Word and the Sacraments (Baptism and the Lord's Supper).

When we say that we are the church of Jesus Christ, does this mean only Lutherans? The answer to this question of course is no. The church is made up of ALL THOSE WHO BELIEVE THAT JESUS IS THE CHRIST, THE SON OF THE LIVING GOD. However, even though we recognize all believers in Christ as fellow Christians and as members of the one Christian church, we cannot be indifferent to teachings that are contrary to the Word of our Lord. We must remember His word to His disciples: "Teaching them to observe all things, whatsoever I have commanded you." (Matt. 28:20)

Now let us talk about the holiness of Christ's church. We confess that we believe in the "holy" Christian church. What does this mean?

The church is called holy because it is the people who are made holy by faith in Christ, and who serve God. The Bible tells us that *Christ also loved the church and gave Himself for it that He might sanctify and cleanse it with the washing of water by the Word, that He might present it to Himself a glorious church, not having spot or wrinkle or any such thing, but that it should be holy and without blemish* (Eph. 5:25-27). Those of us who are the church are already made holy. We are holy because Christ our Lord is holy, and we are "in Him" and part of His body.

In the eyes of God we have been made pure, having no spot or wrinkle, and we are without blemish. This is why we can talk about the holy Christian church. The church has been made clean. The organizations of men are far from clean, and church organizations are far from being holy. But the church of Jesus Christ (or God's people) is holy and acceptable to Him.

III. I believe in "the communion of saints."

What is the communion of saints? As we have seen earlier, communion means "togetherness." The communion of saints is the people of God who are united in Jesus Christ. These people need not know one another, see or talk to one another, or be together, but they are all united to the same living vine, which is Jesus Christ. They are united by God through His merciful gifts. They have the same hope that Jesus Christ is Lord, King, and Savior. They are all praying, "Thy kingdom come," and, "Thy will be done." Most of all, they are ready to share one another's joys and sorrows. They pray for one another. They love one another. They are united in a bond of peace and the living hope that the kingdom of God is come. They know that they belong together for they all belong to God through Jesus Christ. This is what unites them. This is the communion of saints.

So important is the communion of saints that we should think about it over and over again. Often we can feel alone in the world, and sometimes we wonder whether anyone really cares what happens to us. The answer to this question is found in the communion of saints. The church cares about you. God's people care about you. You are never alone. You are one of the many branches which are growing out of the one vine. That vine is Jesus Christ. As your life comes from Christ, so also the life of all Christians comes from Him. This unites you with other Christians, and truly they are your brothers and sisters. While you know but a few of these brothers and sisters, there are millions of them all over the world.

You are united with living brothers and sisters of the faith; more, you are also united with those who have gone on before you. You are also united with Abraham, Isaac, Jacob, Peter, Paul, John, and many others. They also are part of the communion of saints. The fact that their bodies turned to dust does not mean that they are no longer a part of the communion of saints. Death cannot destroy the communion of saints. In the communion of saints there is no death. There is only life. When you confess, "I believe in the communion of saints," you are saying that you belong to the church of Jesus Christ. In this church, people are united and in communion with one another.

IV. I believe in "the forgiveness of sins."

In the very beginning of our studies we talked about "original sin" as the disease with which all of us are born and which separates us from God. Original sin is part of our original condition as we come into this world. Because of original sin, we find ourselves committing various kinds of sins as we go through life. We sin in thought, word, and deed. St. Paul spoke for all of us when he said, "For I know that nothing good dwells within me, that is, in my flesh. I can will what is right, but I cannot do it" (Rom. 7:18).

Since faith in Christ cannot rise by itself, but must feed upon the forgiving Word of Christ, as Luther reminds us, the members of the church pray daily for the forgiveness of sins. In faith we may be confident that God for Jesus' sake "daily forgives abundantly all our sins." Faith never outgrows the need for forgiveness. In fact, faith fastens upon that fact. Through daily sorrow and repentance for sin, and faith in the forgiving mercy of Christ, the Christian becomes a new creature, a new man, every day.

This is what really sustains and upholds the Christian's life. This is what sustains and upholds the church. All our human relationships are burdened and weighed down with our common sin and guilt. The question of guilt is at the very center of life, and its solution is the solution of the whole question of life. It is the most natural and wonderful confession of the members of the church to say, "I believe in the forgiveness of sins." We have "redemption through His blood, the forgiveness of sins, according to the riches of His grace" (Eph. 1:7). "He is the propitiation for our sins, and not for ours only, but also for the sins of the whole world" (1 John 2:2).

Let us think seriously on these things. Let us see that, through Christ, God gives us the forgiveness of sins. Remember the words of the Second Article. *"He* has redeemed me, a lost and condemned creature, purchased and won me from *all sins,* from death, and from the power of the devil; not with gold or silver [has He done this], but with His holy precious blood and with His innocent suffering and death."

But people still ask, "How am I forgiven?" Do I have to feel something special, and will there be a feeling that will tell me that I have been forgiven? The answer is no. You might feel gratitude and also experience the over-powering love of God. BUT YOUR FORGIVENESS OF SINS DOES NOT DEPEND UPON WHAT OR HOW YOU FEEL.

Simply remember that forgiveness comes from God through His Word, which promises you forgiveness. This you may believe with all your heart. What is more, God the Holy Spirit works this faith in you. Cling to the promises of Christ, and go on to live a more Christlike life. Your Christlike life will not earn you heaven, but it will be your thankoffering to the One who has saved you from sin.

V. I believe in "the resurrection of the body."

All of us must die. Jesus also died. He was buried in a tomb. Then He came back to life, but this time His body was different in a strange way which we cannot explain. Even though He still had the marks of the nails in His hands and His feet, and the wound in His side, there was something different about His body.

The Scriptures teach that God on the Last Day will raise us and all the dead. Jesus says, "The hour is coming in which all that are in the graves shall hear [My] voice and shall come forth" (John 5:28, 29). And we are told that our bodies shall not be the same as they are now. Paul says in Philippians 3:21 that Christ "will change our lowly body to be like His glorious body." It seems that Paul thought of our resurrection as being somewhat similar to Jesus' resurrection. Our bodies will then be something different. They will be without the disease of sin. They will not have the seeds of death in them.

On the day of resurrection, Jesus will come with glory, might, and power. "From thence He shall come to judge the quick and the dead."

The day Jesus comes again there shall be a final judgment. At that time He shall separate all people into two groups.

One group shall have the privilege of living with God throughout all time to come (eternity), while the other group will be separated from God forever. See what Jesus has to say about this in Matthew 25:31-46:

"When the Son of Man comes in His glory, and all the angels with Him, then He will sit on His glorious throne. Before Him will be gathered all the nations, and He will separate them one from another as a shepherd separates the sheep from the goats, and He will place the sheep at His right hand, but the goats at the left. Then the King will say to those at His right hand, 'Come, O blessed of My Father, inherit the Kingdom prepared for you from the foundation of the world; for I was hungry and you gave Me food, I was thirsty and you gave Me drink, I was a stranger and you welcomed Me, I was naked and you clothed Me, I was sick and you visited Me, I was in prison and you came to me.' Then the righteous will answer Him, 'Lord, when did we see Thee hungry and feed Thee, or thirsty and give Thee drink? And when did we see Thee a stranger and welcome Thee, or naked and clothe Thee? And when did we see Thee sick or in prison and visit Thee?' And the King will answer them, 'Truly, I say to you, as you did it to one of the least of these My brethren, you did it to Me.' Then He will say to those at His left hand. 'Depart from Me, you cursed, into the eternal fire prepared for the devil and his angels; for I was hungry and you gave Me no food, I was thirsty and you gave Me no drink, I was a stranger and you did not welcome Me, naked and you did not clothe Me, sick and in prison, and you did not visit Me.' Then they also will answer, 'Lord, when did we see Thee hungry or thirsty, or a stranger, or naked, or sick, or in prison, and did not minister to Thee?' Then He will answer them, 'Truly, I say to you, as you did it not to one of the least of these, you did it not to Me.' And they will go away into eternal punishment, but the righteous into eternal life."

The Christian looks forward to this day of judgment, not because he is sure that Jesus might have nice things to say about him, but the Christian knows that the second coming of Christ means the beginning of a new heaven and a new earth.

St. John once had a vision about the new heaven and the new earth. John wrote about it when he was a very old man. Because of his faith in Jesus Christ, he had been turned into an exile on the island of Patmos just off the coast of Greece. There he had a vision of heaven, and his words should be in our minds as we look forward to that wonderful day of Jesus Christ.

> *"Then I saw a new heaven and a new earth; for the first heaven and the first earth had passed away, and the sea was no more. And I saw the holy city, new Jerusalem, coming down out of heaven from God, prepared as a bride adorned for her husband, and I heard a great voice from the throne saying, 'Behold, the dwelling of God is with men. He will dwell with them, and they shall be His people, and God Himself will be with them; He will wipe away every tear from their eyes, and death shall be no more, neither shall there be mourning nor crying nor pain any more, for the former things have passed away.' And He who sat upon the throne said, 'Behold, I make all things new.' Also He said, 'Write this, for these words are trustworthy and true.' And He said to me, 'It is done! I am the Alpha and the Omega, the beginning and the end. To the thirsty I will give water without price from the fountain of the water of life. He who conquers shall have this heritage, and I will be his God and he shall be My son.'"*

VI. I believe in "the life everlasting."

We are absolutely sure that there is a life everlasting. And that it is ours too. What makes us so certain is Jesus' promise. He says,

> *"Let not your hearts be troubled; you believe in God, believe also in Me. In My Father's house are many rooms; if it were not so, I would have told you. I go to prepare a place for you. And if I go and prepare a place for you, I will come again and receive you unto Myself, that where I am, there you may be also. . . . I am the Way, the Truth, and the Life"* (John 14:1-6). *"Verily, verily, I say unto you, He that hears My word, and believes on Him that sent Me, has everlasting life and shall not come into condemnation, but is passed from death unto life"* (John 5:24). *"I am the Resurrection and the Life; he who believes in Me, though he die, yet shall he live, and whoever lives and believes in Me shall never die"* (John 11:25, 26 RSV).

These are the promises of Jesus. He proved Himself to be the victor over death. And He shall make us victorious also.

Our life here upon this earth is important. If it weren't so, God would not have put us here. But there is a life more important than the one we live here and now. This life, then, is a preparation for the life to come. One day God will "raise up me and all the dead, and give unto me and all believers in Christ eternal life. This is most certainly true."

how should I live?

The presentation of Jesus at the temple was chosen to illustrate this chapter. As the presentation at the temple was an act of dedication to the service of God, so is our desire to live according to God's commandments.

THE TEN COMMANDMENTS

The First Commandment

Thou shalt have no other gods before Me.
What does this mean? We should fear, love, and trust in God above all things.

The Second Commandment

Thou shalt not take the name of the Lord, thy God, in vain.
What does this mean? We should fear and love God that we may not curse, swear, use witchcraft, lie, or deceive by His name, but call upon it in every trouble, pray, praise, and give thanks.

The Third Commandment

Remember the Sabbath day, to keep it holy.
What does this mean? We should fear and love God that we may not despise preaching and His Word, but hold it sacred and gladly hear and learn it.

The Fourth Commandment

Thou shalt honor thy father and thy mother, that it may be well with thee, and thou mayest live long on the earth.
What does this mean? We should fear and love God that we may not despise our parents and masters, nor provoke them to anger, but give them honor, serve and obey them, and hold them in love and esteem.

The Fifth Commandment

Thou shalt not kill.
What does this mean? We should fear and love God that we may not hurt nor harm our neighbor in his body, but help and befriend him in every bodily need.

The Sixth Commandment

Thou shalt not commit adultery.
What does this mean? We should fear and love God that we may lead a chaste and decent life in word and deed, and each love and honor his spouse.

The Seventh Commandment

Thou shalt not steal.
What does this mean? We should fear and love God that we may not take our neighbor's money or goods, nor get them by false ware or dealing, but help him to improve and protect his property and business.

The Eighth Commandment

Thou shalt not bear false witness against thy neighbor.
What does this mean? We should fear and love God that we may not deceitfully belie, betray, slander, nor defame our neighbor, but defend him, speak well of him, and put the best construction on everything.

The Ninth Commandment

Thou shalt not covet thy neighbor's house.
What does this mean? We should fear and love God that we may not craftily seek to get our neighbor's inheritance or house, nor obtain it by a show of right, but help and be of service to him in keeping it.

The Tenth Commandment

Thou shalt not covet thy neighbor's wife, nor his manservant, nor his maidservant, nor his cattle, nor anything that is thy neighbor's.
What does this mean? We should fear and love God that we may not estrange, force, or entice away from our neighbor his wife, servants, or cattle, but urge them to stay and do their duty.

The Close of the Commandments

I, the Lord, thy God, am a jealous God, visiting the iniquity of the fathers upon the children unto the third and fourth generation of them that hate Me, and showing mercy unto thousands of them that love Me and keep My Commandments.
What does this mean? God threatens to punish all that transgress these Commandments. Therefore we should fear His wrath and not act contrary to them. But He promises grace and every blessing to all that keep these Commandments. Therefore we should also love and trust in Him and willingly do according to His Commandments.

HOW SHOULD I LIVE?

THE FIRST COMMANDMENT

"Thou shalt have no other gods before Me."

You shall have no other gods before Me. This is God the Father's first law for man. It is His first commandment to you. Jesus said that no other commandment of the Father is more important than this (Matt. 22:36-38). Jesus said that the most important commandment is "Thou shalt love the Lord thy God with all thy heart, and with all thy soul, and with all thy mind."

Now, if you turn to the Book of Exodus (chapter 32), you will see a most amazing thing taking place. Here several hundred thousand people have been saved from slavery. God has saved them. While God was saving them they had seen many of His mighty works. They had even seen the Red Sea open before them just as Pharaoh's armies were about to overtake them. Then they had watched the Red Sea close to devour the best of Egypt's horsemen and chariots. The Children of Israel had been saved by the one true God, but now *they wanted a god they could see*. Anything, even a golden calf, would be all right, so they brought all of their gold to Aaron. They brought rings, bracelets, necklaces, and all other gold in the camp. A huge fire was built, and they melted the gold.

Then they molded the gold and made it look like a calf — like the sacred calf that once was a false god for many Egyptians. When this was finished they threw a wild party. They wanted to make believe that this was a good religious service. The most evil deeds were done. The people acted much like wild animals. They screamed and shouted. Now they had a god, and this god they could see. God, who had saved them from slavery, they couldn't see. This golden calf was better.

They made themselves false gods during the time when Moses was away on the mountain. The goodness of God their Father and of Moses, their great deliverer, was already forgotten.

When Moses came down from the mountain, he was carrying two tablets of stone. On these tablets were written a testimony (a message) from the one true God. The most important message was "Thou shalt have no other gods before Me." But when Moses saw what was taking place, he broke the tablets and then destroyed the golden calf. The golden calf is but one kind of false god and we will look at more false gods later.

But first let us ask the question, "What is the difference between gods (small g), and God (capital G)?"

For one thing we can say that man makes gods, but man cannot make God. You may make a god out of gold. Your god can be yourself (self worship). Your job, your automobile, your power, your popularity, or even another human being can be turned into a false god. *Anything you love and worship more than the one true God is a false god.*

A false god is that certain something in which a person puts his trust before he trusts God. This can be anything or anyone. But only the one true God can give you what is best for you to have. God is true, and for this reason all other "firsts" or "gods" are false. They are false because they cannot save you from your selfishness, greed, and destructiveness. They cannot give you eternal hope and life. Only the true God can do this. He created all things. He keeps all things. He alone is true for He only is God. There is no other god before Him.

In your life here upon this earth, you are always in danger of trying to substitute something or someone for God. This is a common problem for all people. You may spend much of your time worrying about how to be popular with all the people you know. You do this because you want to be liked, and perhaps because you are afraid of not being wanted. But it is important for you to understand that being popular (popularity) is very costly if you seek it. When you want nothing so much as to be liked, then you have a false god, the false god of popularity. You can love this more than God; and if you do, this is putting something before Him. There are thousands of other possibilities for making false gods. Once there was a farmer who had many storehouses for his grain (granaries), but not enough to hold all the crops that came to him. This man had a problem. He decided to tear down all of his old granaries and build new and bigger ones. What for? He says, "And I will say to my soul, 'Soul, thou hast much goods laid up for many years; take thine ease, eat, drink, and be merry'" (Read Luke 12:16-21). He was worshiping a false god. His false gods were wealth and pleasure.

This "rich fool," as he came to be known, probably had spent time standing before his big mirrors admiring his fine clothing. He enjoyed the rich food and good wines that a lot of money can buy. He was "really living," but then he died. The point of Jesus' story is that this man's false gods led him astray. He missed the mark and the purpose for which he had been born. This happens to all people who worship wealth. The rich fool did not reach the full emotional or spiritual growth for which he had been created. He never did become a real man. He could hold his god in his hands, but his god couldn't hold him because it was dead. He had not only cheated God, but he had cheated himself. In place of worshiping the one true God, he had placed his trust, confidence, and hope in things. God says, "You shall have no other gods before Me." The rich farmer died and had to leave all of his possessions behind him. He died without hope. He had not laid up treasures in heaven as Jesus urges us to do (Matt. 6:19-21). Because this farmer was such a fool, he has never been called anything better than the rich fool. His kind of foolishness is very common.

There are many people who don't take the commandments of God seriously. Therefore we might ask just how serious God is about this commandment. God is most serious about it, and you should be thankful that He is. You cannot play around with God. When God says, "You shall not," He means just that. God does not want anyone to misunderstand Him so He tells us straight out, "You shall have no other gods before Me." And we should be thankful that He has let us know what He wants from us. He is God. "I am the Lord your God," are the words He uses. He is to be FIRST in your life. If you try to put Him second to anything, He will turn against your sin. He will do this because He loves you. He knows that your self-made false gods will finally bring you unhappiness and eternal destruction. This is not what your God and Father wants for you. You are precious to Him, and He will stand against anything that might keep you from being His very own.

The First Commandment, like all of the laws of God, is a law of love. Only someone who loves you will give you laws such as God has given. These laws are meant for your good. They are not evil laws, and are not to be feared. God loves you and gives you laws which will help make you a mature person. No one can grow up to Christian maturity if he keeps worshiping false gods.

There is another thing you should keep in mind about the First Commandment. In this commandment God is offering Himself to you. He is saying, "I will be your God," and "you shall be My child." To be His child is your greatest privilege. Everyone needs something or someone to worship. God says, "I am here for you; come unto Me and I will give you rest." He also says, "Have nothing before Me; don't let anything come between us. Put Me first."

Martin Luther explains the First Commandment this way: "We should fear [hold in highest awe and respect], love [give ourselves to], and trust [place our confidence] in God ABOVE ALL THINGS."

We will conclude this discussion with a story. Once there was a man named Saul of Tarsus. Saul knew many things about God. He had studied about God for several years, but for some reason Saul hated many of God's children. He hated the people who followed Jesus Christ. Saul's greatest desire was to bring harm to the Christians. He wanted to see them cast into prison. He wanted the name of Jesus stamped out of the memory of mankind. His anger against the Christians was the most important thing in Saul's life. The anger not only drove and controlled him, but it nearly destroyed him. One day God struck Saul down. (See Acts, chapter 9.) God made Saul blind and helpless. Then God gave him a vision of love and service. Saul's name was changed to Paul. He became one of the greatest Christian missionaries the world has ever known.

Paul suffered much for Jesus Christ. Often he had stones thrown at him, and sometimes was thought to be dead. His friends turned against him because he became a Christian. He was beaten with whips. He was cast into prison. Finally he was put to death. All of this happened to him because he served God above all things. But he still said, "I am the victor. I am the winner." So, remember that God does not promise you a bed of roses if you put Him first, but He does promise that His love will not leave you. "Nothing can separate you from the love of God in Christ Jesus." (Romans 8.) Gladly cast your life on the side of the one true God, for from Him alone comes the gift of eternal life and salvation, and He alone is God.

PRAYER: Heavenly Father, Give me the gift of faith that I might always have the wisdom and courage to put Thee first in my life. May I be like Jesus, in whose name I pray. Amen.

THE SECOND COMMANDMENT

"Thou shalt not take the name of the Lord thy God in vain."

When we think of a friend's name, we at the same time think of that friend as we know him. Even more so, when we hear the name of God, we must think of God Himself, together with everything we know about Him. Whenever we worship and praise the name of God, we worship and praise God Himself. So too, if we take God's name in vain, we dishonor God Himself. This is why the wrong use of the name of God is so great a sin.

There are many people who do not take the name of God seriously. Rather they play with His name as if God did not exist. Some people use the name of God to curse their fellow man, or they may swear falsely while using God's name. They say, "I swear to God that I am telling the truth," when they are telling lies. This is breaking the Second Commandment.

When the name "God" is used, it should be in the most worshipful manner. God is to be talked about, and His name is to be used only with the deepest respect and love. Care and devotion should be used at all times when we speak about God.

When we gather on Sunday morning in the name of the Father, Son, and Holy Spirit, we are gathering before the name of the one true and almighty God, the Father of us all. This should be enough to make one attentive to what is going on at all times. Every minute of the time you spend in church, Sunday school, or confirmation class is in the presence of God. When you say your prayers, you do so in the presence of God. Your entire life is in the presence of God. It is the name of God you are to praise.

Years ago certain people would use the name of God in another vain way. They tried to work magic with the name of God. This was called witchcraft. The name of God would be called upon to do things which were meant to harm other people. This is forbidden in the Second Commandment. However, we can be sure that God is not going to listen to such people. Nevertheless, to use the name of God for any other reason than to thank and praise Him or to ask Him for a loving gift is taking His name in vain. Often God is talked about by people. Perhaps the talk is good. But sometimes there are people who tell off-color jokes in which the name of God is used. This is breaking the Second Commandment. God will not allow His name to be used as a joke. If you have ever engaged in such practices, you had better understand the words of the apostle Paul, "Be not deceived; God is not mocked." (Gal. 6:7)

As a Christian you should always be aware of the wonderful name of God. You should be ready to praise this name above all other names. Nothing should lead you to take His name in vain. Luther said, "We should fear and love God that we may not curse, swear, use witchcraft, lie or deceive by His name, but call upon it in every trouble, pray, praise, and give thanks." When we pray, praise, and give thanks, we keep the Second Commandment.

Finally let us consider the matter of swearing falsely in the name of God. Someday you may be called into court to give testimony. You will be asked to swear before God "to tell the truth." If you tell a lie, you break the Second Commandment. Breaking the commandment of God is most serious, and should your sin be discovered by the court, you will then be accused of perjury. If convicted of perjury (telling a lie under oath) you can be sent to prison. This is serious, but the more serious part of this lying and deceiving is that you are doing it in the name of God.

Another way of taking God's name in vain is to spread false teachings as if they were God's truth. This, too, God forbids when He says, "Thou shalt not take the name of the Lord thy God in vain."

When a Christian uses the name of God, he always does so in a sincere and loving way. The name of God calls for the greatest respect you have to give.

PRAYER: Heavenly Father, may I always keep Thy name holy. Open my lips and lift up my heart in praise to Thy name now and always. Through Jesus Christ my Lord. Amen.

THE THIRD COMMANDMENT

"Remember the Sabbath day to keep it holy."

Many years ago God told His people that they were to set one day aside each week for a very special purpose. This day was to be known as the "Sabbath." On this special day His people were ordered to do no work, but to rest. What is more, they were to set this time aside for worshiping God together as a congregation (gathering) of believers.

The Sabbath came to be the most important day of the week. On that day the Word of God was read and taught to the congregation. The believers came to worship God together, and people made a *special effort* to be with the congregation.

Christians worship on Sunday rather than on the Jewish Sabbath. After the day of His resurrection, Jesus' followers chose Sunday as the most important day of the week because Jesus rose from the dead on Easter Sunday, and because our hope for everlasting life depends on the fact that Jesus rose from the dead on the third day as He said He would. St. Paul says, "If Christ has not been raised . . . your faith is in vain." (1 Cor. 15:14)

As a Christian you will make every effort to be with the members of your church (congregation) on Sunday morning. A Christian will not use weak excuses to miss church. If company comes to your house, you will not stay home from church (as many of today's church members do), but you will urge your guests to go to church with you. God must be tired of hearing people say, "I can't go to church today; I have company."

It is not necessary to talk about the many sorry reasons why people often miss the Sunday worship service, but we must say that God expects the Christian to be in church EVERY SUNDAY. Certain extreme emergencies will sometimes make this impossible, but the Third Commandment means (among other things) GO TO CHURCH EVERY SUNDAY. The Christian's life is to be under the Word of God. He will gladly hear it and live by it.

In the United States less than forty per cent of all church members are on hand for the regular Sunday morning worship service. This is a fact that should make us wonder when someone says that we are a Christian nation. Not even the church members seem to take their Christian responsibilities seriously, or they most certainly would be giving every Sunday to Jesus Christ, who founded the church and died for man's sins.

Some people say that they can be Christians without going to church. This is not likely. There are some sick people who can't get to church because of their illness. But if one can get to church, that's where he will want to be if the love of God and His holy Word means anything to him.

"Remember the Sabbath day to keep it holy." Luther says, "We should fear and love God that we may not despise preaching and His Word, but hold it sacred and gladly hear and learn it."

"That we may not despise." This word "despise" certainly means to look down on with contempt, or even to hate. People might not pay attention to God's Word, and they may not mock it openly. However, many make very little use of the Word of God. This is especially true of those who do not go to church. Luther would call missing church a form of despising God's Word.

God's Word is food to us and for us. Without His Word we die. God's Word is preached by the pastor from the pulpit every Sunday. The church service is built on the Word of God. Therefore preaching and the other parts of the service may be compared to a banquet or a dinner. But if you despise it, you break the Third Commandment, and you hurt yourself.

God serves man and gives him His Word. By means of this Word God gives us His Son and also creates faith to accept Him as our Savior and Lord. This Word is God's gift to you. No other gift can compare with this. If you turn it down, you turn God aside and refuse to make His Word sacred in your life.

Christians would do well to see again how Jesus acted while He was here upon earth. If there ever was a person who didn't need to go to church, it was Jesus. But each Sabbath day He was in the congregation of believers, either as a hearer, or sometimes as the teacher. He prayed with His people, worshiped God the Father with them, and opened the Scriptures to them.

One important reason for going to church regularly is that God wants you to do so. This will sound strange, for what can be more important than a commandment of God? We should go because we are thankful for what God has done for us in Jesus Christ our Lord and Savior. God gave Himself to us in Jesus Christ. God gives Himself to us every day with innumerable blessings. He wills that we should commune with Him in the company of other believers. Going to church is an act of thanksgiving and gratitude to God Almighty. This is the best reason for going to the worship service regularly and for uniting ourselves in common worship of the God who saved us.

PRAYER: Heavenly Father, great is Thy name and greatly to be praised. Give me the holy desire to gather with other Christians to praise Thy name and learn more of Thee. Strengthen and guide my pastor and all pastors everywhere that they may preach Thy Word in truth and purity. In Jesus' name. Amen.

THE FOURTH COMMANDMENT

"Honor thy father and thy mother that it may be well with thee and thou mayest live long on the earth."

When we discuss this commandment, we want to make it clear that this is a law of God.

God commands you to honor your parents. The opposite of honor is to despise, reject, ridicule, mock, etc. Therefore Luther says, "We should fear and love God that we may not despise our parents."

There was once a daughter who always poked fun at her father. She called him many names which amounted to, "Dad you're a dope — a know-nothing — a stupid man." This made him angry. Not only did his daughter despise him, but she caused him to be angry. Luther says that the Fourth Commandment also means, "And do not provoke them to anger." However, this girl showed her father no honor; she offered him no service but expected much from him; she was disobedient and most of her actions were unloving, unkind, and unchristian.

God your Father wants you to honor your parents. You are to realize that God has placed your parents over you, not under you. Many children express a lot of feeling against their parents. To be sure, not all children do this, but one doesn't have to look very hard to see a great amount of disrespect for parents. Therefore we will touch on some of the feelings many young people have toward their parents.

One of the most common feelings is: "My parents just don't understand me." This sounds like a very serious statement. But if perhaps they don't understand, you perhaps do not understand yourself either.

It would be good for you to realize that the early teens can often be an unhappy and confusing age. There are many reasons for this. You are growing and becoming an adult (physically). The chemical changes in your body will upset many of your feelings. For a few years you may be mixed-up, and during this time your judgment will not be as good as it might be. This poor judgment might make you believe that your parents are at the root of all your problems. This could be true, but generally it is not. For when you grow up, you may discover that your father and mother were much wiser than you had believed them to be.

No matter what you feel or think, what counts is that God says, "Honor your father and mother." What does honor mean?

(1) To honor means to show proper respect to someone who has authority over you; hence, that you be willing, or ready, to obey him. You obey those whom you honor. If you honor God, you obey Him. Such obedience you are to give your parents, for God has given them to you as your protectors until you are an adult and has given them authority over you as His own representatives. (Note: We cannot consider the problem of obedience to parents who make unchristian demands upon their children. Problems such as these call for personal consultation with the pastor.)

Obedience also covers the minor daily requirements of household chores such as cleaning up your room, doing the dishes, helping with the meals, and mowing the grass. Obedience is the acceptance of decisions about the hours you keep, where you go, and with whom. You will like this least of all, but your parents are responsible for you; and if they are concerned about you, they will certainly have rules and regulations you are in duty bound to observe. If you think that they are unreasonable, it might be well to have a "quiet" talk with them; or perhaps you would like to go and tell your pastor. Maybe he can help clear the problem for you and help your parents understand what you mean and want.

But whether you talk to your parents or pastor about your feelings, you must understand that God commands you to be an obedient child. Maybe you don't care for a flat statement like this. Perhaps you will say, "No one is going to tell me what to do." But God is telling you what to do because He loves you. He wants you to honor your parents for His sake.

(2) There is such a thing (rather common) as false, or counterfeit, obedience. An example of this is to make life miserable for the one to whom you are pretending to give obedience. You may be asked to scrub the kitchen floor. You hate the job, forgetting that you are helping your mother. Then perhaps you discover that if you do a poor

job she will think it easier to do it herself. So you slough off and do it so badly that Mother finally gives up and does it herself.

Your action is positive disobedience. This is dishonoring your mother. Another way of not showing honor is complaining when you are asked to help. Complaining is a favorite pastime. Hearing a person complain makes one think that inside he is a child who does not really want to grow up. You might decide that because the Fourth Commandment demands obedience, you will do just what the law asks, but no more. True honor is co-operative and goes beyond what you are asked to do. So, if you honor your parents, you will find new and better ways of being more co-operative every day. Even as Jesus gladly helped Joseph in the carpenter's shop, so also Christian young men and women respond with love and respect to the needs of their parents.

As a Christian you will avoid all unchristian behavior toward your parents. Honoring parents means to be truly obedient and co-operative. This is the most rewarding way for you to live. However, don't expect your parents to be perfect. They never are, nor are you. Only God is perfect. But whether they are perfect or not, God says, "Honor thy father and thy mother that it may be well with thee." It is well with the person who follows this very important law of God.

Now we must carry the Fourth Commandment another step. It applies to anyone who has authority over you. This means the government, teachers, pastors, and all others in such position. You must remember that when you provoke a teacher to anger, you are committing sin. A Christian will have no part in this kind of behavior. You owe your teachers honor, respect, obedience, and co-operation.

Martin Luther's explanation of the Fourth Commandment is not difficult to understand. It is straight to the point. He says, "We should fear and love God that we may not despise our parents and masters, nor provoke them to anger, but give them honor, serve and obey them, and hold them in love and esteem."

PRAYER: Heavenly Father, forgive me for being unfaithful to this commandment. Enable me to behave as a Christian should, and inspire me to love and honor my superiors. Through Jesus Christ my Lord. Amen.

THE FIFTH COMMANDMENT

"Thou shalt not kill."

This is one of those commandments a person might want to hurry over. Most of us have never killed anyone, and we don't intend to do so. But Martin Luther saw more in the Fifth Commandment than murder, and he got this understanding from Jesus, who made this law read deeper than the physical act of murder.

The first thing about the commandment is that God forbids killing another human being. Just what this means for a man whose country asks him to fight in a war is another question. For now we will consider the act of murder as it is commonly understood.

What makes murder wrong? Not only that the laws of the land (government) forbid it, but, more important, that the Law of God forbids murder.

The first murder is pictured in the Book of Genesis. Here we find Cain killing his brother Abel. Since the first murder there have been millions more.

Murder is possible because in all people there is a violent side. There is that part of the personality which is ready to hurt and destroy others. The Bible, as well as scientific psychology, states this fact. In most of us this destructive side is covered up, and in some people it is almost entirely hidden. But in all people there is some kind of violence. People are born that way. You are born with original sin. You must be saved by Christ from sin, and you must learn to love rather than to kill.

While people do not generally kill one another, they often find ways of bringing harm to their neighbor. In other words, something short of murder. This happens when gangs of hoodlums attack defenseless people. The newspapers tell about these things. The Fifth Commandment also includes hurting or harming our neighbor.

The Bible teaches that hatred and murder are the same thing. "Anyone who hates his brother is a murderer." (1 John 3:15.) In other words, if you wish that someone were dead or wish that some evil would fall upon him, this is the same as murder. Hatred always carries the wish that the hated person be destroyed. If you hate someone, you really wish that person to be dead, and therefore you are a murderer. As a man thinks in his heart so he is.

Murder is a most serious crime of man. In some states murderers are executed while in others they are put in prison for life. The civil law of man establishes several kinds of murder such as first, second, and third degree. But whether murder is in thought, word, or deed, it is sin against God, who says, "Thou shalt not kill." We are to help and befriend our neighbor in his need. Read the parable of the good Samaritan (Luke 10), and you see the opposite of murder.

PRAYER: Heavenly Father, help me to love my brother at all times. Forgive my lack of love. May I do my brother no harm. Through Jesus Christ my Lord. Amen.

THE SIXTH COMMANDMENT

"Thou shalt not commit adultery."

To commit adultery means, in the first place, to be unfaithful in marriage. It means, in the second place, to have sexual relations without being married. It means even the desire for sexual relations without being married. It means finally to think impure thoughts, to speak unclean words, and to look at obscene pictures.

Let us begin by saying that God meant men and women to choose someone from the opposite sex with whom they want to live until death separates them. When two people make this decision, they usually announce their engagement. They are now engaged to be married. Everyone is supposed to understand that one of the most important choices of life has been made by two people who have declared their love for each other.

In Christian circles the engagement also means that this choice of lifelong mates has been blessed by God. What is more, in the eyes of God a promise made by one person to another is sacred and meant to be kept. Therefore one should not take his or her engagement promise lightly.

Preparation for marriage begins at a very early age when the child is being taught important lessons. If the child is to grow up and have a happy marriage, he or she certainly must be taught how to be considerate, kind, generous, and loving, because these personal qualities are necessary for a happy marriage.

Christians teach their children that God demands His people to be pure in mind and body. Jesus said, "Blessed are the pure in heart, for they shall see God" (Matt. 5:8). The pure in heart are those who are saying to God: "Thy will be done in me."

God's will for most people is that they should be married. Many people for one reason or another never get married, but this is the exception rather than the rule.

Happy marriages are most possible for people who have made certain decisions long before they get married. The most important decision is that they will remain pure. Such persons will not enter into any relationships with members of the opposite sex which God meant to be reserved for marriage only.

Most of the time adultery takes place because people allow themselves too many other liberties, such as petting. Adultery, although serious, can be forgiven. Once Jesus took the side of an adulterous woman. When others wanted to stone her to death Jesus forgave her sins. Although adultery can be forgiven, it often leaves some bad wounds in the personality. There are people who are not able to forget that they committed adultery. It is not the kind of sin from which one can find quick relief. If one does not take the commandment seriously, he or she may discover one day that much of the personality has been harmed. It is much better to come to the altar with a pure mind and a pure body. What joy one has when he can take his loved one and say, "I am yours only; I have never given myself to another."

God wants you to give yourself to one person in marriage until death. Giving yourself to more than one person is adultery. This is the concern of God's Sixth Commandment.

As a Christian you must learn how to REJECT behavior that is unchristian. You must learn how to say No. No one can really argue with the courage to say no although some persons will try to do so. You can say, "God does not want me to do that." This kind of courage to be what God wants you to be will draw respect from most people.

Up to this point we have been thinking most about the actual act of adultery. Jesus gives us another interpretation of the commandment which seems rather difficult. He said that a person can commit adultery by having adulterous thoughts that are pointed at another person (see Matt. 5:27, 28). This is the "impurity of thought" with which Jesus deals. This is a problem far more difficult than the first.

So much of your everyday life is surrounded by direct attacks upon your thoughts. Advertising is heavily loaded with powerful sexual appeals. Motion picture stars and starlets often allow themselves to be photographed in such ways that they create great adulterous desires in people. Also there are many magazine publishers who aim the full strength of their publications at the sex drives of people who are frustrated and unhappy. This attack on the structure of our civilization has been so serious that in some states laws have been passed to prohibit the sale of such literature.

What then is a Christian's responsibility when he or she is surrounded by such great evil? *The Christian has an answer, but the answer is not one of great fear.* Some Christian leaders say that we should all be wearing blindfolds, or that we ought to be like the three little monkeys. These three little monkeys sit in a row. One has his hands over his eyes, one is plugging his ears, and the third monkey is holding his hands over his mouth. The motto is, "See no evil, hear no evil, speak no evil." But we cannot walk down the street or drive cars with blinders on our eyes. We cannot keep our ears plugged. However, we can refuse to speak evil. We can reject all impurity which will in any way cost us dearly in the years to come. Your mind is one of the finest gifts God has given you. Your Christian responsibility is to reject all that will corrupt your mind and to take hold of that which is good. There is so much good for you to have. There is good literature, good motion pictures, and good television. There is the world of science and the study of many subjects which can increase the powers of your mind. You can be of use to other people and most of all to the kingdom of God. The world is so full of good things. You can reject that which is evil and still have so much to do that there is no time to spare. You can also take advantage of good recreation and learn how to play as a Christian. You can work as a Christian, and you can choose Christian companions.

The very best thing you can do is to be a disciple of Jesus Christ. This alone is enough to give you all of the necessary things of life. Jesus said, "Seek ye first the kingdom of God . . . and all these [good] things shall be added unto you" (Matt. 6:33).

But, as a Christian you must always look at the facts. Most people (including young people) feel the urge to express themselves in a sexual way. And as they think about this urge they become disturbed. It is not wise for you to try to run away from them, or bury them deep in your mind. When you do this you "repress" or push under some very powerful forces which can cause you pain and confusion later on in life. It would be much wiser to understand that such urges are "natural" (meaning that they are built into you) and *repressing them is not getting rid of them.* You must first look at them. You must find someone (preferably your parents or pastor) with whom you can talk. Sex stirrings should be looked at like blood pressure, digestion, or any other physical function of the body. Once it is understood that the sex urge is intended by God to find its expression within the bounds of holy matrimony, the fear that it is evil will vanish.

Finally, you should pray. God knows, long before you tell Him, about the struggles going on within you. But it is good for you to say: "Father, forgive me my impurities, and remake me in Jesus' name."

In conclusion, remember that because He loves you God has commanded you to "keep thyself pure." Martin Luther used these words to explain this commandment: "We should fear and love God that we may lead a chaste [clean] and decent [good] life in word and deed, and each love and honor his spouse [husband or wife]." Let us also note that smutty jokes about sex are not for the Christian, but all reference made to this blessing of God will be pure and wholesome.

Your marriage is to be for life. Never forget this. This makes it important for you to be prepared for marriage and the blessings it can bring. Start making the important preparations now by making the important decision to keep yourself for the one you are to marry.

PRAYER: Heavenly Father, create in me a clean heart, and renew a right spirit within me. By Thy most gracious power keep me pure, and make me faithful to Thee and the one I am to wed. In Jesus' name I pray. Amen.

THE SEVENTH COMMANDMENT

"Thou shalt not steal."

Most people realize that stealing is wrong. People cannot live together in harmony if stealing is allowed. If stealing were allowed, the strongest would destroy the weak. There could be no government, everyone would be constantly threatened by his fellow men, and man would live in great fear.

God gave the Seventh Commandment because He wanted a group of people to live together in harmony. A nation needs laws to protect people from other people. One very necessary law is "Thou shalt not steal." This means that we shall not "take our neighbor's money or goods, nor get them by false ware [deception] or dealing, but help him to improve and protect his property and business."

The Seventh Commandment is divided into two parts. (1) You shall not steal, and (2) You shall help.

You shall not steal. We do not have to say too much about this. If you take something from your neighbor that does not belong to you, and if your neighbor (be he the one next door, or any other human being) does not know what you have done, and if he would not have given it to you unless you had paid him for the property — if you take what does not belong to you, you are a thief. If you are a thief, you break the Seventh Commandment of God. Taking something from someone without his consent or knowledge is certainly stealing. Let us now think about less obvious kinds of stealing.

For instance, there is cheating. This occurs in school whenever you manage in some way to get grades you could not otherwise receive without more hours of study. Or you can agree to work for a certain wage, and then not give the best of the services you have promised. This is one of the most frequent kinds of stealing, and it has come to the point where many persons take pride in the fact that they are able to get paid for the work they have not done. Collecting excessive insurance claims is stealing. Often people do this. Giving someone a wrong impression about the quality of goods sold to him is stealing. We could go on and on. We live in an age when this kind of stealing is thought of as being shrewd and smart business, but God condemns this as a transgression against His law: "Thou shalt not steal."

You shall help. This certainly is a Christian responsibility. So often when people see their neighbors and friends getting things, they are envious. Some people get quite bitter about such things. There are always people who will do almost anything short of murder to destroy what their neighbors have done or gained. But the Christian rejoices over the blessings his neighbor enjoys, and the Christian helps his neighbor improve his property and business.

But we should know that God owns all things. We should not be confused about this. Nothing really belongs to man. Man is only "permitted" to use certain things. Man is given the right to use time in which to work and play — talents such as his physical strength and mental capacities, and resources such as money and property. For proof of this see the parable of the talents (Matt. 25:14-30). You will understand from this story that man has nothing he can call his own or "mine." Therefore the Christian will not say "mine." The Christian always says, "It is God's property and I am to take care of it for Him."

Many years ago the prophet Malachi spoke out against his people because they had forgotten that all things belong to God. They promised to give God the best lambs of their flock. But when the time came to do this they took the sick lambs, the worst of the flock, and offered them to God. They kept what they had promised to give to God. They broke the Seventh Commandment.

All of your life should be an offering to God, or you are stealing from Him. Surely He wants you to use what He gives you, but He never wants you to forget that all He gives is still His. To help you remember this truth, God has established acts of worship such as bringing regular offerings for the carrying on of His work here upon earth. But as it is, man does not like the idea until he has learned better.

Every year far more money is spent for entertainment than for the work of God's kingdom. People spend time and money for things that give them pleasure, but when asked to give offerings to God, they often hesitate. Most often God does not come first; He comes last, if at all. This is not true for the Christian. The Christian puts God first and at the very top of his budget. That portion dedicated to God is taken out before anything else is attended to. Each Christian decides what percentage of his income this shall be, but whatever he gives, he gives because he has recognized that all he has belongs to and comes from God. The Christian does not attempt to steal from God. You have time, talent, and resources. These are not yours to have but only to use. Someday you must lay them all aside. You cannot take them with you when you die. On the day of judgment (see the parable of the talents) God will ask you, "What have you done with My possessions?" And then you will have to give an answer. How sad it would be if you would have to say, "I spent them (His talents) on myself. I sought what I thought was happiness. I had much, but I gave so little." Then you will stand before the God of all creation exposed as a thief. Malachi asked, "Shall a man rob God?" Man should not, but he tries.

Your talents, mind, body, and possessions, are meant to be used for the kingdom of God. Always remember that Christians are persons who know that God is Lord over all things.

God the Father has withheld nothing from you. You break the Seventh Commandment when you hold back from Him. Even worse, when you steal from God, you take His many loving blessings and throw them aside as though they counted for nothing.

PRAYER: Heavenly Father, may I not steal from Thee or my fellow men. Make me able to give and keep me from the wrong of taking from others or keeping for myself what belongs to Thee. Through Jesus Christ my Lord. Amen.

"Thou shalt not bear false witness against Thy neighbor."

This law deals with such commonly accepted evils as gossip. It warns us not to "deceitfully lie about, betray, slander, nor defame our neighbor." It also urges us to "defend him, speak well of him, and put the best construction on everything."

As a Christian you have a direct responsibility toward your neighbor, and your neighbor is any other human being, regardless of his race, creed, or color. (See the parable of the good Samaritan, Luke 10:25-37.) "You shall not bear false witness [tell a lie about] any other human being." This statement is straight to the point and there is no excuse if you make an exception to this law of God.

To bring to light the meaning of this commandment, let us choose a few examples. The use of such words as "nigger," "gook," "wop," "kike," or any other similar expression is forbidden. Ill words directed toward other people are acts in which the Christian cannot share. Irresponsible talk about anyone is a crime against God and man. Persons who slander their neighbors often fool themselves into believing that their evil acts are good. Isaiah said, "Woe to those who call good evil, and evil good" (Is. 5:30). Such people think up some "righteous" cause to cover their deeds of sin. They will say, "I have nothing against so and so — BUT," and then they go on and say all sorts of evil things about that individual. Such people as these will take a rumor about a person and tell the story as though it were true. Their hatred is fired up, and they become the most evil of all people.

Even Jesus had to suffer from such evils. People told lies about Him. (See Matt. 26:59-61.) False witnesses were used against Him before He was sentenced to death. James says, "Speak not evil one of another, brethren" (James 4:11). Also read Ps. 50:19-22, Luke 6:37, or Matt. 18:15.

In Matt. 18:15 Jesus tells us how we should behave if we have anything against our neighbor, and every Christian should read these words carefully.

Certainly the Christian Church cannot allow gossip and false witness to go unrebuked. The Church is to be a community of believers, a true "brotherhood." In this community we are to share one another's joys and sorrows. We are not to gossip or backbite. Christians should have the courage to tell the gossiper they will have nothing to do with such evil. What is more, the Christian will urge such individuals to go to the person they are offending and tell how they feel and what they think. This takes courage.

Gossipers are cowards. There is nothing that is more certain than this. If they had courage, they would take their complaint to the one against whom they have grievances. They do not do this. The dark deeds of evil flee from the light.

Our blessed Lord suffered much at the hands of cruel persons who attempted to make evil out of the good He was doing. All Christians will certainly experience the same burden, but Jesus says, "Love your enemies and pray for those who persecute you" (Matt. 5:44). When the Christian is attacked, he does not return evil for evil. This is what is so different about him. The Christian tries to understand the cruel actions of his neighbor against him. While he will hate the evil his neighbor does, he will also pray for the gift to love and help the one who persecutes him. Jesus is the example. When He was on the cross, He was still able to pray for His tormentors, "Father, forgive them, for they know not what they do." (Luke 23:34)

Lies and slanders against another person may seem innocent, but they never are. Such behavior is always evil. It is always sin against God and our fellow man. Jesus said, "The second [commandment] is . . . Thou shalt love thy neighbor as thyself." [1] (Matt. 22:37-40)

If you are guilty of breaking this commandment, you can be healed but (1) you must see your behavior as sin, (2) you must confess your sin to God, (3) if at all possible you must make right the wrong you have done by confessing your sin to the one you have wronged. This sounds difficult, but there is no easy answer to such sins as these. God is ready to forgive you. He will also give you new courage to be decent and honorable in all things. He

---

[1] This commandment "Love your neighbor as yourself" is very interesting. We know that many people have not learned how to like or love themselves. If a person cannot accept himself (as God accepts him) then he very likely is also unable to accept or to love others.

will help you love yourself more and then you will not want to hurt others.

As a Christian you are asked to "put the best construction on everything." This means that when you hear something evil about another person you make every attempt to learn the truth. You do not add evil to evil. You understand that there may be much that is still unknown.

We must also understand that keeping silent can be a sin. Many times Christians make the mistake of being silent when they should speak up for someone who is being slandered. This can be just as bad as repeating the story. Silence does not discourage evil.

There is no greater waste of time than gossip and slander, nor is there much that is more destructive to one's own personality. Life is too short to waste by gossip or slander. God calls you to enter the fellowship of love. "Love one another as I have loved you" (John 15:12).

PRAYER: Heavenly Father, help me to control my tongue, and give me the power to speak good of my brother. Through Jesus Christ my Lord. Amen.

THE NINTH AND TENTH COMMANDMENTS

"Thou shalt not covet."

Commandments Nine and Ten deal with the same problem, that of wrongfully wanting something which belongs to one's neighbor. Commandment Nine states the general law "Thou shalt not covet," and Commandment Ten gives more examples.

We live in a day when things such as money and clothes are very important to people. However, people have always had this problem. Many people lay up their treasures here upon earth. They measure their success by the things they are able to buy. The size of the bank account, home, auto, and TV set seem to tell the story of success or failure. Grasping for things is a disease, and it runs deep in the heart of our society.

Grasping for things causes discord. Some people get very uneasy when a neighbor begins to get more things than they have. Envy and ill feelings develop. Sometimes friendships break up because one person gets more than the other. Often people want what belongs to their neighbor, wanting it at his expense.

Such wanting what belongs to one's neighbor is sin, and God speaks against it in these final two commandments.

The sin of covetousness has caused pain for many people. King David was nearly ruined by this evil. David wanted another man's wife and got her by having her husband placed in the front lines of a military battle. The woman's husband was killed as David had intended, and then David took his wife. (See 2 Sam. 11:2-27)

When people begin coveting what other people have, private wars break out. When nations covet what belongs to other nations, then international wars break out. As Christians we already have far more than any amount of money can buy. The priceless gift of salvation through Jesus Christ is more than all the goods of the world can supply. To some people this sounds like foolishness, but for the person who has been given life in Jesus Christ there is no need to wish for more.

It is wonderful to be genuinely happy when someone else gets something new, but even more important, it is wonderful to see that in Jesus Christ we have far more than the whole world can give. The Christian is so thankful for God's love that he does not have the time nor desire to become anxious about what he might not have. Therefore do not covet what belongs to your neighbor. Be thankful for the many blessings God has already given you. You are rich. God loves you.

PRAYER: Heavenly Father, give me grace and a thankful heart so that I need not envy my neighbor nor covet what is his. Through Jesus Christ my Lord. Amen.

THE CONCLUSION TO THE COMMANDMENTS

"I, the Lord, thy God, am a jealous God, visiting the iniquity of the fathers upon the children unto the third and fourth generation of them that hate Me, and showing mercy unto thousands of them that love Me and keep My commandments."

Sin is born in us and is passed on from one generation to another. Many kinds of evil are passed along from generation to generation. Selfish parents will usually rear selfish children. Cruel parents very often will rear cruel children, and parents who do not worship God will bring up children who do not worship God. For three and four generations and more, this chain reaction can continue if something doesn't happen to stop it.

God says, "I am a jealous God," or, "My glory I will not give to another." The Bible shows us very well that God will not permit anyone to take what belongs to Him. For those who break the commandments He has given, there is a severe warning. God wants us to know that He does not overlook sin. God is merciful to those who love Him and keep His commandments.

The evil man should be afraid of God's laws, for God will destroy all evil. The Christian will thank God for His commandments. God does not keep His people in the dark. We know what He expects of us, and what He has given us. We would be in a dreadful state if God had not spoken to us through His Law and Gospel.

But God has spoken to us. None of us can claim to be ignorant of what God wants. We know what God wants, and each of us must take personal responsibility for his own conduct in life. If we choose to do evil, we cannot blame God. If we take God's power to do good, we will give all credit to Him and thank Him for giving us the power of the Holy Spirit so that we are able to do that which is good. (See Article Three of the Apostles' Creed.)

We live in a day when some people are trying to find more and more reasons why persons should not be held responsible for their own behavior. This is all right in the cases of some who have lost control of their minds. But for the most part we must believe that man is responsible and is to be held responsible for what he does or fails to do. Still there are those who saw that man is a slave to his surroundings (environment) and therefore must be excused for the evil he does. However, St. Paul says that men "are without excuse" (Rom. 1:20). You and I are held personally responsible for all sin we commit. But the Bible promises, "If we confess our sins, God is faithful and just to forgive us our sins and to cleanse us from all un-righteousness." (1 John 1:9)

We have now concluded our study of the Ten Commandments. But this is just the beginning. No one can study the Ten Commandments and let it go at that if he wants something important to happen in his life. We must try to live the Commandments. By the power of the Holy Spirit we can grow every day into a new richness of life if we will keep these ten rules in mind and write them upon our hearts. Surely we will meet with many failures, but we will also meet with some success. Most of all, we will grow toward greater Christian maturity.

Day by day you are faced with problems. The answers to these problems are often difficult. When you are tempted to take the easy way out, or to make hasty decisions, it is good to remember that your character develops as you decide and act.

In the Ten Commandments, God has given us a set of rules to guide our decisions and actions. All that we decide to do affects our personality one way or another. As we make decisions, and as we act, we need a standard to help us decide what is right and what is wrong. The Ten Commandments are this standard. Certainly we are always going to be tempted to break the Commandments, and it is not always easy to recognize temptations when they come. But if we keep the Commandments in mind, we shall be more able to do that which is right. We will begin to understand that by keeping the Commandments we do loving actions. We express our love for God and our fellow men by being obedient to God.

The Ten Commandments forbid unloving actions. Sometimes these actions seem remote from our lives. For instance, we seem far away from the commandment which tells us that we should not kill. However, the discussions concerning the Ten Commandments have pointed out that when one decides to cheat on an examination, one has actually decided to steal. To try to understand this and decide not to cheat (steal) may make it easier, later in life, to decide to be honest to an employer, honest with one's family and friends and, most of all, honest with God. To try to live according to the Ten Commandments is not easy. It might help to remember that, while they are commandments, they are at the same time guides to show us the many temptations to do unloving acts. They therefore help us avoid doing things for which we would undoubtedly be sorry.

PRAYER: Heavenly Father, I take personal responsibility for my conduct and behavior. I turn to Thee for the forgiveness of my sins. May I live for Thee. I thank Thee for the Commandments. In Jesus' name. Amen.

how should I pray?

In the illustration for this chapter Dürer shows Jesus praying. We have the example of Christ before us. Through Jesus Christ we are children of God and may pray "Our Father."

THE LORD'S PRAYER

The Introduction

Our Father who art in heaven.
What does this mean? God would by these words tenderly invite us to believe that He is our true Father and that we are His true children, so that we may with all boldness and confidence ask Him as dear children ask their dear father.

The First Petition

Hallowed be Thy name.
What does this mean? God's name is indeed holy in itself; but we pray in this petition that it may be holy among us also.

The Second Petition

Thy kingdom come.
What does this mean? The kingdom of God comes indeed without our prayer, of itself; but we pray in this petition that it may come unto us also.

The Third Petition

Thy will be done on earth as it is in heaven.
What does this mean? The good and gracious will of God is done indeed without our prayer; but we pray in this petition that it may be done among us also.

The Fourth Petition

Give us this day our daily bread.
What does this mean? God gives daily bread indeed without our prayer, also to all the wicked; but we pray in this petition that He would lead us to know it and to receive our daily bread with thanksgiving.

The Fifth Petition

And forgive us our trespasses, as we forgive those who trespass against us.
What does this mean? We pray in this petition that our Father in heaven would not look upon our sins nor on their account deny our prayer; for we are worthy of none of the things for which we pray, neither have we deserved them; but that He would grant them all to us by grace; for we daily sin much and indeed deserve nothing but punishment. So will we also heartily forgive, and readily do good to, those who sin against us.

The Sixth Petition

And lead us not into temptation.
What does this mean? God indeed tempts no one; but we pray in this petition that God would guard and keep us, so that the devil, the world, and our flesh may not deceive us nor seduce us into misbelief, despair, and other great shame and vice; and though we be assailed by them, that still we may finally overcome and obtain the victory.

The Seventh Petition

But deliver us from evil.
What does this mean? We pray in this petition, as the sum of all, that our Father in heaven would deliver us from every evil of body and soul, property and honor, and finally, when our last hour has come, grant us a blessed end and graciously take us from this vale of tears to Himself in heaven.

The Conclusion

For Thine is the kingdom and the power and the glory forever and ever. Amen.
What is meant by the word "Amen"? That I should be certain that these petitions are acceptable to our Father in heaven and are heard by Him; for He Himself has commanded us so to pray and has promised to hear us. Amen, Amen, that is, Yea, yea, it shall be so.

HOW SHOULD I PRAY?

Christians learn how to pray to God their Father. Jesus prayed, and when the disciples asked Him, "Lord, teach us to pray" (Luke 11:1), Jesus gave them the Lord's Prayer. If you could pray no other prayer than this; if you knew no other words to use in making your approach to God; and if you prayed this prayer several times each day, you could not use up the meaning and depth of this prayer. Jesus gave us a deep blessing when He taught this prayer.

Martin Luther divided the Lord's Prayer into nine parts. We will study the Introduction, the Seven Petitions, and the Conclusion.

THE INTRODUCTION TO THE LORD'S PRAYER

"Our Father who art in heaven."

What does this mean? "God would by these words tenderly invite us to believe that He is our true Father and that we are His true children, so that we may with all boldness and confidence ask Him as dear children ask their dear Father." (Martin Luther)

Jesus has asked us to open this prayer by calling God "Our Father." Our blessed Lord wants all of us to know that God is not just like a good father to us, but that God is really the Father. He is the Creator of the world and all that is in it. God is the Giver of life. He has given life to you. Truly, He is your Father, and when you pray you are to say "Our Father." You are to turn to the Father with faith, *confidence and trust*.

You are a child of God. Never forget this. You can always say "Our Father." Jesus told a story to help you remember that God is a loving Father (Luke 15:11-32). It is the story of a boy who forgot and then remembered again that he had someone to whom he could say "Father." Our Lord wants you to remember that God loves you. You can ALWAYS pray the prayer Jesus has given you.

"Our Father" is the introduction to the prayer which Christ has given His church. Even when you pray alone, it is good to say "Our Father." You can also say "My Father," but this prayer wants to say that God is the Father of all with whom we are united in Jesus Christ, our Lord. While you are calling upon God the Father, there are thousands of other believers doing so also. At the moment you start your prayer, a man in China, India, or Africa may be saying "Our Father." Persons with different-colored skins and different languages are united under the same God, and they pray "Our Father." When you pray the Lord's Prayer, you are united with other believers. You agree that not only are you a child of the same Father, but that they also are your brothers and sisters.

You cannot use the Lord's Prayer if you carry unchristian thoughts about how you or your race is better than another. Only if you have seen that you are a brother or sister to everyone who believes in God through Jesus Christ — only then are you able to say "Our Father."

The "Our Father" is for you to use, but it belongs to the group, or the church. It is a prayer for the whole Christian church to be praying together. It is a prayer which speaks of the unity between God and man, and man and man. The "Our Father" prayed by the church of our Lord can unite our hearts and lives and help destroy misunderstanding that exists between us. No opening sentence of a prayer can be more important, more wonderful, or more powerful than "Our Father."

God is above everything that you can see or touch. He is greater than anything you can imagine. He is above all things. He is "in heaven." Although He comes to you in this world and meets you where you are, God is not tied to this earth. He holds the earth "in the palm of His hand." Where is God? God is in heaven. God is beyond all that you know which is good. This is heaven.

"Who art in heaven" — by praying these words you confess that God is greater than any person or power. "Heaven" is your way of saying that God is almighty and above all creatures of the earth. This should remind us of God's fatherly love toward us and of His unlimited power to hear our prayer.

So the Introduction comes to an end. We turn now to the Seven Petitions. These are seven things for which you ask God in this prayer. Things asked for are called "petitions."

THE FIRST PETITION

"Hallowed be Thy name," or: May God's name be kept holy in all places and at all times. "God's name is indeed holy in itself; but we pray in this petition that it may be holy among us also" (Martin Luther). In other words, "Help me to keep Thy name holy in my life at all times and in all places."

How is the name of God to be kept holy? (See the Third Commandment.) "When the Word of God is taught [in church, Christian day school, Sunday school, home, etc.] in its truth and purity and we, as the children of God, also lead a holy life according to it" (Martin Luther). Surely this is the main desire of every Christian. May you always make God's name "hallowed" in your life by hearing His Word, learning it, and keeping it. May nothing in your life mock or ridicule His name. He is your Father. May you pray, "Hallowed be Thy name."

THE SECOND PETITION

"Thy kingdom come." The first message Jesus gave to man was: "The kingdom of God is at hand. Repent ye [turn from your old ways of sin]" (Mark 1:15).

Every kingdom has a king. God has a kingdom. Christ Jesus our Lord is the Lord of this kingdom. Jesus calls this kingdom "Mine" and said, "My kingdom is not of this world" (John 18:36).

Christians know that the most wonderful kingdom is the kingdom of God. Christians also know that in order to be in the kingdom of God, the kingdom of God must first be in the person. You are in God's kingdom because God is in you through His Holy Spirit. But the kingdom is only "in you" in a very small way. Your faith and love for God, your desire to serve Jesus Christ, and your willingness to give your life to that which is good, is small. Your faith is like a little grain of mustard seed. This seed must grow every day, or it will die. This faith is given to you by the grace of God through His holy Word. Your faith can grow only if it is protected by God's power and fed by His love, which comes to you through His holy Word.

Praying this petition calls for people who have courage, for the kingdom of God is unlike anything else in this world. When the kingdom comes to you, you start to be different from the people in whom the kingdom is not. You are now interested in the plan of God for you. You are now concerned about the things which belong to His kingdom. While other people give themselves to the things of this day and this world, such as wealth, power, and popularity, the Christian is concerned about the kingdom of God coming among men.

As the Bible teaches, the kingdom of God will move on to final victory. In fact, it is already victorious. No men or nations can stop it from coming. Your purpose in praying this prayer is to ask God to make His kingdom keep coming in you also.

But you are asking more than "Thy kingdom come in me." You are also praying that God will make His kingdom come to all people in all the earth. You will do this because Jesus has asked you to be concerned about all other people. Jesus said, "Go ye into all the world and preach the Gospel" (Mark 16:15). So in this petition you are asking God for the grace to want other people to be brought into His kingdom. Your prayer will not stop with the words "Thy kingdom come," but you will help send missionaries into all the world to tell people the kingdom of God is at hand. If you are not interested in bringing the Gospel of Jesus Christ to all creatures, you are not really ready to pray, "Thy kingdom come." One day the kingdom of God will reveal itself in all its glory. On the last day of this world the Lord Jesus will come in His heavenly majesty and every knee shall bow, and every tongue shall confess that Jesus is Lord to the glory of God the Father. (Phil. 2:10)

THE THIRD PETITION

"Thy will be done on earth as it is in heaven."

In this petition we pray as Jesus did in the garden of Gethsemane on the night He was betrayed. God has loving desires for you. He has a definite purpose for your life. He desires that you will accept His plan for you. When you pray this petition, you are asking your loving Father in heaven to take your life into His hands and do with it just as He pleases. Even as all of the angels in heaven are completely under God's rule, so you also desire to be subject to Him here upon earth and in heaven.

God's will is done perfectly in the kingdom of heaven, where there is no evil to prevent the good. But here upon earth there is much evil which prevents the good will of God from being done perfectly in you. This evil is called sin. Sin stands against God's will for you. Sin wants to destroy you, while the will of God is meant to give you eternal life. The will of God for you (see Second Article) is that you should be God's child, "live under Him in His kingdom, and serve Him in everlasting righteousness, innocence, and blessedness."

You must understand that God's will for you will separate you from much that you might have come to know and to like. If you ask God to do His will in you, then you give Him the right to make decisions for you. You give God the right to decide what you shall be and where you shall go. He will be Master of your life. This you ask when you pray, "Thy will be done on earth as it is in heaven."

Once again, however, your prayer is not just for yourself. You are also praying that the good and perfect will of God shall be done in all men. No Christian prayer is ever purely directed or meant for one's self alone. It always includes all men. This is true for the Third Petition of the Lord's Prayer, where you ask for the will of God to be done on earth, or throughout the entire earth, or among all men.

The big problem for many people is this, "What is the will of God for me?" Although we have already given an answer to this question, we must understand that the answer is given in many other ways by other people. For instance, there have been terrible cruelties committed by persons in the name of God and His will. This has been done in the organized church where people have been tortured, imprisoned, and put to death in the name of God. This happened during the times of the inquisitions and the witch-burnings. Even today there are evil people who say that they are doing the will of God when they are being unkind, unloving, and cruel. We might wonder what the will of God may be for us.

The Christian knows one thing for certain about the will of God. He knows that it is God's will for him to be saved. He knows that his life should be filled with love and goodness. He knows he is to be given faith and courage to live a Christlike life. Finally he will be taken to heaven to live eternally with God. The Christian can always be certain of this. Beyond this the Christian must always pray, "Thy will be done," and then believe that God will answer this petition. God will certainly answer you. You have no way of knowing just how God will answer your prayer until He lets you know. But you can be sure that your loving Father will take hold of your life and give it a holy direction which will make you a true "saint" in His kingdom.

THE FOURTH PETITION

"Give us this day our daily bread." Here Jesus tells you to ask God the Father for food and also for all other things you need. Our Lord always wants you to understand that such things as food come from God. Too often people are confused about this. They think that food comes from man. But when you realize that food depends upon rain and sunshine, and that a seed of wheat or corn cannot grow unless God gives it life, then you know why you should pray, "Give us this day our daily bread."

Two purposes of this petition are to help you be thankful for your daily bread and to help you remember that God is the Giver. This thankfulness should always be expressed in regular table prayers before you eat. The Christian realizes that God gives him his daily bread, and for this he says, "Oh, give thanks unto the Lord, for He is good, and His mercy endureth forever." God wants His children to understand that He is the Giver.

Many years ago, when the Children of Israel were wandering about from place to place in the desert (see Book of Exodus), God kept them alive by giving them bread and water. Each day they came out of their tents to gather the food their Lord had given them. They were commanded to take only as much as they needed for one day. Many of them doubted that God would feed them on the next day. Because they lacked faith in Him, they tried to take more than they needed. But God let their surplus food spoil. He wanted His people to trust Him every day for their daily bread.

In the Fourth Petition you do not ask for more food than you need, nor for special kinds of foods. Certainly food is very important, but God does not want you to be overly concerned about it. If you are too concerned about food, you lose concern for the needs of your spirit. Jesus asks the question, "Is not life more than food?" (Matthew 6: 25). People who live only for their stomachs are never able to be great persons. They would rather stuff their stomachs than enter the kingdom of God. When you watch them eat, you see that "their god is their belly" (Phil. 3:19). Jesus asks us to be content and to believe that God will give us enough food to keep us alive. If you have faith, you will not be anxious about what you shall eat or drink or put on. Jesus says, "Your heavenly Father, who clothes the lilies of the field and feeds the birds, will also feed and clothe you" (Matthew 6:28-33). We must also give a word of warning. God expects us to work for what we eat. The "give us" part of the prayer does not mean that daily bread will come to us if we are sluggardly and lazy. God gives us the resources with which food can be produced, but we are expected to work. The land must be tilled. The crops must be sown. The harvest must be taken. Man must earn his daily bread, but he can do this only because God gives him the power to produce the things necessary for life.

THE FIFTH PETITION

"And forgive us our trespasses, as we forgive those who trespass against us."

Perhaps there is nothing in the Lord's Prayer more direct and powerful for us than this petition. Here we ask God for the forgiveness of our sins. Trespasses means "sins." To trespass means to go where you are not permitted to be, or to do what you are not allowed to do. Most of all we should be concerned because every day by thought, word, and deed, we grieve and offend our God and Savior. Often we also trespass or sin against our neighbor by unloving and unkind acts. Furthermore we are sinned against by other people. All of this leads to hard feelings and conflict and people doing wrong to each other. When such wrongs grow, they result in hatred, bloodshed, and murder on a big scale. The Christian is concerned that wars, big and small, should stop.

Praying the Fifth Petition is a way to help stop hatred and war. But so often the words of this petition are treated lightly. Many people will speak the words without caring about what they are saying.

Now let us look carefully at these words. First we must see that the translated words (from the original Greek text) can be read two ways. (1) "Forgive us our trespasses (or debts) *as* we forgive those who trespass against us." (2) "Forgive us our trespasses, *FOR* we forgive those who trespass against us." Either of these two meanings is valuable to us.

If we take the first meaning (1), we are asking God to forgive us only if, and when, we are forgiving those who are wronging, or have wronged us. This puts a responsibility upon us. If we do not forgive, how can we think that God will forgive us? Scripture agrees. Our Lord said, "With what measure you measure, it will be measured to you again" (Matt. 7:2). Therefore it is right to believe that only as you forgive will you be forgiven. (See also the story of the unjust steward, Luke 16.)

Turning now to the second meaning (2), we see that it is taken for granted that Christians are forgiving people, and therefore they can say, "Forgive us, for we forgive those who trespass against us." This is really true for the followers of Jesus Christ. Christians have heard the Lord say to them, "Love [keep on loving] one another, even as I have loved you," or, "Keep on forgiving one another even as I forgive you." But some of the greatest Christians get mixed up about this. Even Simon Peter did.

One day Simon Peter was very much concerned about this matter of forgiveness. He wanted Jesus to answer the question, "How often shall I forgive my brother if he sins against me? Seven times?" (Matt. 18:21). This, to Peter, was a grand offer because the religious leaders of the day said that when a man forgave his neighbor three times he had done more than was required of him. By saying "seven times," Peter may have expected the Lord to tell him, "Very good, Peter." But the Lord didn't say, "Very good Peter." The Lord said, "Seven times seventy times," or, "You shall always be forgiving." This is to say that the person who sets a limit to his forgiveness is not behaving as a disciple of the Lord.

Day by day you are faced with the words which you pray in this petition. Day by day you have opportunities to be kind, forgiving, and loving. You are not to be the person who says, "I forgive him or her BUT." There is to be no holding back of your forgiveness. You are not to hurt or harm the one you say you have forgiven. You are not to carry resentments, hatred, or a grudge against him. Jesus sets the example when He prays for His enemies. "Father, forgive them, for they do not know what they are doing" (Luke 23:34). This is what forgiveness means.

Forgiveness also means forgetting evil. God says, "I will not remember your sins" (Isaiah 43:25). And the psalmist says, "As far as the east is from the west, so far does He remove our transgressions from us" (Psalm 103:12). If you stop short of putting away from you the memory of the hurt done to you, you fail the Fifth Petition, you fail yourself, and your Lord. God has cast your sins away from Him. He has healed you by forgiveness in Jesus Christ. Our sins put Jesus on the cross, but we are forgiven. We are to forgive because we have been forgiven. May God grant you the grace to pray the Fifth Petition.

THE SIXTH PETITION

"And lead us not into temptation."

Certainly God does not tempt any person to do evil. God leads people to be good if they will follow Him. Our prayer in this petition is that God will keep us so securely in His care that we will not be tempted to forsake Him and do evil. We also ask Him to guard our faith so that we do not lose our trust in Him.

The Sixth Petition can be understood better when you understand it as part of the Third Petition. If you have prayed, "Thy will be done in me," you have turned your life over to God. "The Lord is my Shepherd, He leads me. . . ."

If you have ever been blindfolded and then asked to allow another person to lead you, you know that this can make you anxious. However, if you could be led by the same person for a long time, you would learn to trust him. That is, if you were not led into harm or danger. Being led by God is something like wearing a blindfold. This does not mean that you walk in darkness, for you certainly don't. But it does mean that the things which used to guide you no longer do. Now God guides you. His will leads you.

As you pray in the Third Petition, so in the Sixth Petition you are asking God not to allow you to fall from Him into evil or, "Do not lead me into such a place where I become afraid and am tempted to leave Thee. I am weak. Don't ask me for more than I am able to do. Keep me in the shelter of Thy wings. I want to be Thine alone. Don't let anything change this. Don't put me in a position where the choice I must make is too difficult. I am weak in my faith and can panic and sin. Help me never to be tempted to deny Thee as my God and Savior, and Lord."

THE SEVENTH PETITION

"But deliver us from evil."

As we have noted before, evil is very real in this world. Evil always seeks to destroy the good. Satan does not rest from his attempt to take complete control of the world God the Father has created. In Matthew 4:1-11 (see the

Sixth Petition) we see that Satan did not hesitate to attack the Lord. However, when he failed with Jesus, he did not give up his plan for destruction. Judas Iscariot, the apostle Paul, and every disciple of Jesus Christ has had to face this evil power. Some, like Peter and Paul, gain the victory. Others, such as Judas Iscariot, fall deeper into sin and forsake their God and Savior.

You, too, are a target for the devil. The more you seek to be good and to do good the more you can expect to be met with the temptation to do evil. Those people who are truly concerned about doing what is right are especially attacked by the devil. The "fence sitter" or the person who doesn't take a stand for anything is not bothered much by the vicious attacks of Satan.

You are a target, too, of "the world," that is to say, the unbelievers, the Christ-haters. As you take your stand to be a true Christian, you cannot expect to be spared. Jesus was not spared, and He warned His disciples not to hope that they would have the special privilege of "being delivered from evil." Rather He promised them that they would have to face much from evil men. (Matt. 10:16 ff.) You find, too, that there are stirrings within you, sometimes called your "own sinful flesh," which urge you to do evil. These also you have in mind when you pray, "Deliver me from evil." In sum, when you pray the Seventh Petition, you are beseeching God, your heavenly Father, to deliver you from any and every kind of evil that might destroy your body or spirit. You are asking your heavenly Father to give you the resources *to reject evil and choose the good.*

You should also understand that the Christian "takes up his cross" (Matt. 16:24) and follows Jesus. He is ready to suffer for Jesus Christ as Stephen (see Acts 7) and many others did. The Christian does not say, "Because I must suffer, I know that God does not love me." The Christian knows that he must suffer many things (Acts 14:22). But do not confuse suffering with evil. Suffering is not always evil. Suffering for the sake of your Lord is not harmful; it is good. Also it is not hurtful to suffer in order to become what God wants you to be, it is good. *The prayer of this petition is not to deliver you from suffering, but you pray to be delivered from evil.* This point is so important that every Christian should understand it completely.

There are many false prophets who say that all suffering, physical and otherwise, is evil. They tell people that God hates suffering. God certainly does not like suffering, but He gave His own Son for the sins of mankind (John 3: 16), and in this act of love for His children, God suffered terribly. Who would dare say that the suffering of Jesus was evil? The sins that made His suffering necessary are evil. The men who crucified Him were evil men. His death was not evil; by dying He paid for our sins. This was good. Any suffering for the sake of God and His kingdom is good. In the Seventh Petition you are not asking God to deliver you from suffering, but you are turning to God for the strength to meet evil with faith and courage for final victory.

THE CONCLUSION

"For Thine is the kingdom and the power and glory forever and ever. Amen."

You have come to the end of the Seven Petitions. Now you add the Conclusion.

In the Conclusion (usually called the Doxology), you again look up into the heaven, as you did in the Introduction. You ascribe to our Father the kingdom and the power and the glory.

You now give *reasons* why God should hear your prayer. You say, *"For* Thine is the kingdom." You say in effect: "Thou art a king and dost act as does a king. Thou art the great Ruler over everything." You say also, *"For* Thine is the power." Nothing is impossible for our heavenly Father to do.

And you conclude, "For Thine is the glory." As you receive mercy and help from your heavenly father, especially daily forgiveness of your sins, daily renewal of your faith, daily strength to walk in His ways, you praise and glorify His holy name.

More. Your doxology is a *confession.* "Thine is the kingdom" — not the devil's. In all the ups and downs of life, you steady yourself on this pillar of truth.

"Thine is the power." No matter how brazenly the anti-Christian governments of today are flaunting their power before the face of God and man, "He who sits in the heavens laughs." He will "dash them in pieces like a potter's vessel." (Psalm 2:4, 9 RSV)

"Thine is the glory!" You confess that your petition will be heard by God, not only for your sake, but also for the sake of the glory your Lord derives from granting them. Finally, the doxology is a *pledge*. You promise allegiance and give it promptly and loyally. You accept the new order of things in your Lord's marvelous kingdom. "All hail the power of Jesus' name . . . and crown Him Lord of all!"

"Thine is the glory!" Christ would cast the demon of selfishness from your heart. He would knock, enter, and take possession of it, so that you might shape all your actions to enlarge the glory of God. You live and work in God's sunlight. You, who were created in the image of God, are in the darkness of sin, but when touched with the glory, the light of God, you also shine and sparkle in the glory of God.

There shall be no end! Forever and ever you shall glorify God. You shall be able to take hold of the real purpose for which you have been born. You will glorify God without any temptation to take His glory from Him. You shall be one with the Father and live in perfect harmony with Him. *Amen,* or yes, this is so. I believe what I have said, I agree. This I confess to be true.

The Lord's Prayer is the perfect prayer. In it is to be found everything necessary for you, but you will also want to pray other prayers.

Always remember that you can come to God in prayer at any time and for anything and everything. Do not be afraid to ask God for the things you want. However, always close your prayers with "Not my will but Thine be done." You might be asking for things which will do you more harm than good. But never let this possibility stop you from asking. Ask, firmly believing that God will answer your prayer in a way which is best for you. St. Paul prayed that God would remove severe sickness from his body. God never granted him this request but gave him instead new and greater spiritual gifts, over which Paul rejoiced. (2 Cor. 12:7-10)

In this illustration the risen Christ extends His hand to fallen man. This is a direct representation of the grace of God which comes to us through Christ and His Church.

The Office of the Keys and Confession

It is the peculiar church power which Christ has given to His Church on earth to forgive the sins of penitent sinners but to retain the sins of the impenitent as long as they do not repent.

Confession embraces two parts. One is that we confess our sins; the other, that we receive absolution, or forgiveness, from the pastor as from God Himself and in no wise doubt, but firmly believe, that by it our sins are forgiven before God in heaven.

The Sacrament of Holy Baptism

Baptism is not simply water only, but it is the water comprehended in God's command and connected with God's word.

The Sacrament of the Altar

It is the true body and blood of our Lord Jesus Christ under the bread and wine, for us Christians to eat and to drink, instituted by Christ Himself.

I LIVE BY GRACE

THE OFFICE OF THE KEYS AND CONFESSION

I. The first question we shall ask is: What is the Office of the Keys?

It is the peculiar (special, particular) power which Christ gave His church on earth to preach the Gospel, whereby the forgiveness of sins is offered to men in His name. This power includes the right to hold back forgiveness when there is no repentance and confession of sin.

On Easter evening when our Lord appeared to His disciples in the upper room, He said, " 'Peace be with you; as the Father has sent Me, even so I send you.' And when He had said this, He breathed on them, and said to them, 'Receive the Holy Spirit. If you forgive the sins of any, they are forgiven; if you retain the sins of any, they are retained.' " (John 20:21-23 RSV)

When Christ did that, He made the church, and in it our brother, a blessing to us. Now our Christian brother stands in Christ's stead by His command and promise to say to us, "I declare unto you the forgiveness of your sins in the name of the Father, and of the Son, and of the Holy Ghost. I loose you before God." Or our Christian brother has the power to stand before us and say,

"I do not declare unto you the forgiveness of all your sins. I bind you before God." In St. Matthew's Gospel our Lord also said, "Truly, I say to you, whatever you bind on earth shall be bound in heaven, and whatever you loose on earth shall be loosed in heaven." (Matt. 18:18 RSV)

Our Christian brother would not have this power if Christ had not given it to him. He hears the confession of our sins in Christ's stead and he forgives our sins in Christ's name. He keeps the secret of our confession as God keeps it. When we confess to our Christian brother, we are confessing to God, too. So when in the Christian fellowship we confess and we forgive, the grace of God is at work in us and through us, one to another. But if our brother will not repent of his sin nor confess it before God, he cannot be forgiven.

This function, or office, of loosing or binding, of forgiving or retaining sins, IS GIVEN TO THE CHURCH. In its broader meaning it includes the power, or authority, to preach the Word of God, to administer the Sacraments, and especially the power to forgive and to retain sins. The sins of the penitent sinners are to be forgiven. Penitent sinners are sinners who feel sorry for their sins (contrition) and believe in Jesus Christ as their Savior (faith). But the sins of the impenitent sinners, that is, of those who are not sorry for their sins and do not believe in Jesus Christ, are to be retained as long as they do not repent.

Martin Luther said that every Christian has the power of the keys, that is, the power to forgive sins or to retain them, but that no one should exercise this power in the name of others (the congregation) unless authorized to do so. All Christians have this power, but not all are elected or called by the congregation to use it. The pastor of the congregation uses the power of the keys in the exercise of his ministry on behalf of or in the name of all. The pastor may loose (declare forgiveness), or he may bind (withhold forgiveness) as he acts in his office. When the congregation has decided to exclude someone from its membership, the pastor will carry out the resolution of the congregation. He will exclude the sinner from the rights and privileges of a Christian.

Christians are God's people because of Christ. In Him the love of God comes to the sinner. The righteousness of Christ covers all sin. In this sense, God's people are a devout and holy community. People of the world hear this phrase, "God's holy people," and they do not understand what it means. They look only on the surface of the lives of Christians and they say, "They are not that good." But they don't understand the real quality of the Christian life which "is hid with Christ in God." This does not mean that Christians do not have problems with sin. As Luther says in the Small Catechism: "For we daily sin much and indeed deserve nothing but punishment." Christians do not try to hide or deny their sin and guilt. That would be hypocrisy. All men are sinners, Christians included. All men need the forgiving mercy of God. The main thing in the Christian life (and we might say, the special mark or quality of the Christian life) is the confession or acknowledgment of sin and the acceptance in faith of the grace and forgiveness of God for the sake of Christ. God's people trust only in God for the forgiveness of sins. They seek and pray in faith for what God will give them in Christ.

Therefore, the church of Jesus Christ, knowing herself to be His body, a fellowship of redeemed and sanctified people with a distinctive mission to perform, is to be deeply concerned that nothing within the body shall defile her members, undermine her life, limit her witness to the world, or endanger the fulfillment of her mission. The church is very conscious of the fact that all her members are sinners and that her life is not perfect. She knows that this sinfulness in the individual or in the congregation hurts her life and her work. But she knows, too, that there is abundant grace to cover this sin where daily sorrow, repentance, and faith rise up to claim it. The mark of the Christian and of the members of the church is not perfection but penitence and faith. Where there is no repentance and confession of sin, there the life of the church and her fellowship are harmed, her witness to others is weakened, and her work is hindered. The church must always be on guard against those who do not repent.

This is important when we remember that the church has the call and commission to "go into all the world and preach the Gospel." The church is to bring men and women and children into the kingdom of God through the preaching and teaching of the Gospel. The church also has the divine command to discipline and train the disciple. The church has the task of safeguarding and sustaining the life of the disciple under the Word of God. As a member of the church, you have this responsibility to yourself and your fellow Christians.

It may happen in the church that one of its members will no longer show the quality of the Christian life — repentance and faith. In other words, by his life and in his spoken words he will not admit to sin and accept forgiveness. If he refuses to repent after the members of the congregation have done everything possible to admonish him and get him to see his sin and his need of forgiveness, they must cease fellowship with him. The Christian fellowship must speak out to every sinner who will not repent and confess his sin and seek forgiveness; and it must confront him with the choice of what he loves most: his sin or Christ. If he hears the pleas of his brothers and repents of his sin and accepts in faith the forgiveness of Christ, there is rejoicing. If he will not hear the pleas of his brothers and persists in his sin, there is nothing else to do except put him out of the congregation in the hope that he will see his sin and repent. This passage of Scripture has great force and meaning: "My brethren, if anyone among you wanders from the truth and someone brings him back, let him know that whoever brings back a sinner from the error of his way will save his soul from death and will cover a multitude of sins." (James 5:19 RSV)

II. Now we ask the question: What is confession?

Confession embraces two parts. The first is what we do, that is, when we sorrow over our sin and lament it, desiring the assurance that the broken relationship with God be restored and that we be forgiven. The second part is a work which God does when He absolves us of our sins. That we are forgiven may be an assurance which we have by faith in the Gospel. This assurance may be given by another person who speaks the Gospel to us. It is good for us to hear the Gospel on the lips of our Christian brother when he speaks to us in the name of Christ.

Now, we know that there are several kinds of confession. There is (1) confession to God alone. This confession is absolutely necessary. St. John says, "If we say that we have no sin, we deceive ourselves, and the truth is not in us. If we confess our sins, He is faithful and just, and will forgive our sins and cleanse us from all unrighteousness" (1 John 1:8, 9 RSV). The writer in the Book of Proverbs says, "He that covereth his sins shall not prosper: but whoso confesseth and forsaketh them shall have mercy" (Prov. 28:13). This confession the true believer is always making.

There is (2) confession to another person alone when we have done him a wrong. This confession is also of divine command. See Matt. 5:22-26; Luke 15:18.

There is (3) confession to a Christian brother or pastor who will receive us for Christ's sake and give us the word of consolation and forgiveness from God. This confession is not demanded, but it is a good thing to do.

To the first kind of confession we give expression in the Lord's Prayer when we say, "And forgive us our trespasses as we forgive those who trespass against us." Indeed, the whole Lord's Prayer is a confession that we neither have nor do what we ought; and it is a plea for grace and a happy conscience. This kind of *general* confession should and must take place again and again as long as we live. We acknowledge that we are sinners and pray for God's grace.

We may make the *private* confession to a Christian brother or to our pastor. It may happen that we are especially burdened by a certain sin. We may feel that it is a sin which cannot be forgiven. Our conscience may hurt terribly, and God and His promises of forgiveness may seem to be for everyone else but not for us. The devil may urge, "Your sin is too great to be forgiven." When this happens, it would be a good thing to talk this over with your pastor. You may confess the particular sin which burdens you. You do not have to. You may simply confess that you have sinned, that you confess this sin before God, and that you seek the forgiveness of God and through your pastor the assurance that you have forgiveness from God. Always remember the words of David: "I acknowledged my sin unto Thee, and mine iniquity have I not hid. I said, I will confess my transgressions unto the Lord; and Thou forgavest the iniquity of my sin." (Psalm 32:5)

Many times sin will burden us and we will desire to hear the words of forgiveness. As any pastor can tell you, there are many people who come seeking someone to tell them that they are forgiven. They wish the Gospel to be spoken to them in the words of a Christian brother. They come confessing their sins, and are cheered and relieved to hear someone in Christ's name assure them with these words: "As a called and ordained servant of the Word, I declare unto you the forgiveness of all your sins in the name of the Father, and of the Son, and of the Holy Ghost." When one receives such absolution, he may be sure that he is forgiven just as certainly as if Christ had spoken to him Himself.

Private confession is not demanded, but we are free to use it whenever we need it. In fact, we are not to despise private confession, for with it we receive the blessing which the absolution gives. To unburden our souls, to get it off our chests, as we say, to speak out and confess our sin is good. Our sin is revealed and judged as sin and we hand it over to God. This is all good. However, the absolution (assurance of forgiveness) is the important part. This is the work of God. When we make use of the privilege of private confession, therefore, we do it primarily because of the absolution which the pastor gives. In Christ's name he receives you and in the name and in the stead of Christ he forgives you. We should remember that the forgiving and loosing Gospel is upon the lips of our Christian brothers by Christ's command and promise.

Confession is, in a true sense, discipleship. In confession the Christian forsakes his sin and seeks his life in Christ. What happened to us in Baptism is bestowed upon us anew in confession. In the sorrow of repentance the old man in us is drowned, and in faith in Christ the new man comes alive. As sinners we are to die daily by contrition and repentance and come to life by faith. This is no good work on our part, however. It is only God's offer of grace, help, and forgiveness that would make us dare to stand with our hearts bared before God in confession. We can confess solely for the sake of the absolution.

Members of the body of Christ, to which you belong, are a "society of the concerned." They are always concerned about firming up the sagging loyalties of those who become weak and neglectful of the means of grace.

"Brethren, if a man is overtaken in any trespass, you who are spiritual should restore him in a spirit of gentleness. Look to yourself, lest you too be tempted. Bear one another's burdens, and so fulfill the law of Christ. For if anyone thinks he is something, when he is nothing, he deceives himself. But let each one test his own work, and then his reason to boast will be in himself alone and not in his neighbor. For each man will have to bear his own load. . . . So then, as we have opportunity, let us do good to all men, and especially to those who are of the household of faith." (Gal. 6:1-5, 10 RSV)

HOLY BAPTISM

We have learned that God acts to save us when we are helpless, unable to do anything to save ourselves. We believe that He forgives our sins for the sake of the sacrifice of His Son, Jesus Christ. When we are born, we are dead already in sin, actual enemies of God. Our sin separates us from God. Unless we are changed we shall always be separated from God.

That God acts to take away our sin and guilt by the power of His love and grace will become clear to us as we study the teachings of the Bible on Holy Baptism. The Christian Church teaches that Baptism is very important. And it is. When we are baptized we are made children of God. God makes us His children by a new spiritual birth. He makes us members of the body of Christ, gives us the Holy Spirit, and makes us heirs of eternal life. All this God does for us in Holy Baptism.

How do we get all of this in such a simple thing as Baptism? How does Baptism do such great things? The answer is: Because Baptism is not merely water; but it is water embraced in the Word and command of God. The water which we use in Baptism is connected with the Word and command of God. In Baptism we apply water to the person being baptized and say as we do it, "I baptize thee in the name of the Father, and of the Son, and of the Holy Ghost." This is exactly what Jesus told us to do. And God uses this simple means to make His act of saving the world a present reality for each of us.

God uses Baptism as a "means of grace," a channel through which His grace comes to us, a way by which He "offers, conveys, and seals" to us individually the forgiveness of sins which Christ has earned for the whole world by His sinless life and His innocent suffering and death on the cross.

It is God's Word which makes Baptism much more than a handful of water. God's command makes the act of Baptism much more than a trifling matter, "like putting on a new red coat," as Luther said.

Before Jesus ascended into heaven, He gave His disciples a commandment. He told them: "Go therefore and make disciples of all nations, baptizing them in the name of the Father, and of the Son, and of the Holy Spirit, teaching them to observe all that I have commanded you; and lo, I am with you always, to the close of the age" (Matt. 28:19, 20 RSV). This is His word of command.

In this word of command we need to understand one word more clearly — "baptizing." To baptize simply means to wash something (or someone) by sprinkling water on it, pouring water over it, or putting it under water (immersion). If in Baptism we put water on the person in any of these ways, we are doing what Christ commands.

We might ask at this point, Who is to do the baptizing? Well, to whom was Christ speaking when He gave His command? To His disciples, His followers, in other words, to His church, to all Christians. Now, although every Christian has the right to administer Baptism, there is in most church denominations, for the sake of good order, a chosen representative in charge of baptizing. This is the pastor who has been called by the congregation. But if there is an emergency, if an unbaptized person is near death and no pastor is on hand to do the baptizing, you or any other Christian should do the baptizing. Simply put some water on the person's head, and say the words given to us by Jesus: "I baptize thee in the name of the Father, and of the Son, and of the Holy Ghost." But always remember that this is a Sacrament, an official sacred act of the church. If at all possible, Baptism should take place in the house of worship with the pastor administering the Sacrament.

We note, too, that Christ commanded to baptize "all nations." Who, then, should be baptized? Everyone that hasn't been baptized. Children, too? Certainly; they are just as much a part of "all nations" as men and women are. But some people, some churches, do not believe in baptizing children. They argue that because children are too young to know what is going on, they should not be baptized. This is not a good argument, because there are a lot of things about which the Christians can't know. For instance, we can be told about the love of God, but we can't understand it. Does this mean that we stop believing in the saving love of God? These same people who will not baptize children talk about the need for faith, but they do not have faith enough to believe that God can actually grant His grace through the Baptism. Therefore, since Jesus told us to baptize all nations, who are we to decide that Jesus didn't mean children? *For God, Baptism is an act of grace. For us, it is an ACT OF FAITH.*

But do infants really need to be baptized? Are they not born pure and innocent? St. Paul tells us that we "were by nature [from birth] the children of wrath" (Eph. 2:3), that we were "dead in trespasses and sins" (v. 1). This is why Jesus told Nicodemus, "Truly, truly, I say to you, unless one is born anew, he cannot see the kingdom of God. . . . Unless one is born of water and the Spirit, he cannot enter the kingdom of God. That which is born of the flesh is flesh, and that which is born of the Spirit is spirit." (John 3:3, 5, 6)

So we see the need for bringing children to God in Baptism. Jesus said, "Suffer the little children to come unto Me, and forbid them not; for of such is the kingdom of God." This is why Lutherans, Catholics, and some Protestants believe that children should be brought to Jesus in Baptism. And when the child is baptized, his sins are all washed away, and he becomes a citizen of the kingdom of God. He belongs to God and has an inheritance belonging to him — eternal life in heaven. And when the child is older, he will be told about this inheritance.

That this is true about Baptism, both for children and for adults, Luther declares when he answers the question: What does Baptism give or profit? Or, what are its gifts and blessings? He says: "It works forgiveness of sins, delivers from death and the devil, and gives eternal salvation to all who believe this, as the words and promises of God declare."

Our Lord's word of promise is in the last chapter of Mark: "He that believeth and is baptized shall be saved; but he that believeth not shall be damned" (Mark 16:16).

St. Paul says that "according to His mercy He saved us by the washing of regeneration and renewing of the Holy Ghost, which He shed on us abundantly through Jesus Christ, our Savior, that being justified by His grace, we should be made heirs according to the hope of eternal life. This is a faithful saying." (Titus 3:5-8)

Because Jesus has commanded us to baptize in the name of the Father, and of the Son, and of the Holy Spirit, we Christians take His commandment very seriously. Though we cannot understand how Baptism can forgive sin, give new life, make one a child of God and a member of Christ's kingdom, we believe what the words and promises of God tell us. In obedience to His command and trusting in His promise the church baptizes children in His name. St. Paul assures us, "You are all children of God by faith in Christ Jesus. For as many of you as have been baptized into Christ have put on Christ." (Gal. 3:26, 27)

Luther reminds us that "to be baptized in the name of God is not to be baptized by man but by God Himself." If we are to come into His kingdom, we must be brought in by God Himself in the way that He has commanded. We trust the "sign" of our Baptism, that is, the application of the water with the Word, which sacrament becomes for us a "gracious water of life and a washing of regeneration in the Holy Ghost."

Thus far we have stressed that Holy Baptism is God's Word and action which once and for all gives Christ to us. Yet Holy Baptism is a process, an ongoing action which extends throughout our entire earthly life. The Christian life is a "perpetual Baptism," as Luther calls it. What is he talking about? He is talking about the "significance" (or meaning) of Baptism.

In the Small Catechism Luther describes the ongoing meaning of Baptism. He said, "Baptism signifies that the old Adam in us is to be drowned and destroyed by daily sorrow and repentance, together with all sins and evil lusts; and that again the new man should daily come forth and arise, who shall live in the presence of God in righteousness and purity forever."

In one of his sermons Luther also explained this when he said, "The Sacrament or sign of the baptismal rite is soon over, as we see with our eyes. But the significance, the spiritual Baptism or the drowning of sin, lasts all our life and is not completely accomplished until our death."

What Luther is saying is that Baptism gives us the great privilege of being children of God; but it also means that we are to live and act as God's children.

In other words, in our Baptism God concludes a covenant with us, sinners though we are. That is to say, He enters into a personal fellowship with us while we still are sinners. He becomes our Father and we become His children. Though there will always be sin in our life, it cannot condemn us because of our faith in Christ, which is counted to us for righteousness and makes us His children.

Yet we remain sinners who must fight our remaining sin all our life through acts of repentance and faith. Daily we are to be sorry for sins and ask God for Christ's sake to grant us forgiveness and strength to do God's will alone. The old man in us should daily become weaker and gradually die. The new man in us should daily grow stronger. This is the significance of our Baptism. This is the life of faith in Christ which our Baptism implies.

The real meaning of Christian Baptism, then, as we believe, is much more than that which we see when a person is being baptized. If we think that this is something we have to do just because others are doing it, then we are mistaken. If Baptism is nothing more than giving the child a name, then there is no purpose in it. You can name a child without baptizing him. Or, if we stop at the point of Baptism, believing that God is acting only for this moment, we are missing the point again. We must always see Baptism as a gift from God which takes us through our whole life. The power of Baptism goes with us every day and even into our grave. The power that is in our Baptism also raises us from the dead on the Last Day. The gifts of Baptism go with us into eternity. The covenant promise of God is that He will be our God and we will be His people forever.

Since God is faithful to His covenant in Baptism, we pray that God will keep us faithful through His Word. Our study and use of God's Word is never done. In church services, in Bible classes, in home devotions, our life is to be lived under the Word of God.

The Word of God embraces our life in the baptismal covenant, and the Word also is to touch our life again and again in the spoken and visible Word in preaching, teaching, and the Holy Communion.

THE SACRAMENT OF THE ALTAR

It would be good to understand the various names by which this sacrament has been described. Other than "The Sacrament of the Altar," the most commonly used names are "The Lord's Supper," "The Holy Communion," and "The Holy Eucharist." Why these names?

1) The sacrament was instituted or originated by our Lord Jesus Christ while He and His disciples were eating the Passover supper. Therefore the term "The Lord's Supper."

2) The sacrament is a communion (a union of one thing with another) of the bread and wine with the body and blood of Christ. It is also a communion (participation) of believers with Christ and with one another. Therefore the term "The Holy Communion."

3) The sacrament is also a "feast of thanksgiving." Our Lord gave thanks when He instituted the sacrament and as Christians "do this in remembrance of Christ," they do it with thanksgiving. Therefore the term "The Holy Eucharist." (The word is from the Greek and means "giving of thanks," or "thanksgiving").

4) The sacrament is usually administered at the altar in the church; therefore the term "The Sacrament of the Altar."

I. Why did our Lord Jesus Christ institute the Sacrament of the Altar and command Christians to "do this in remembrance" of Him? It happened the same evening He was betrayed. The words of institution are important. While observing the Passover festival with His disciples, commemorating the deliverance of the Children of Israel from bondage in Egypt, Jesus "took bread; and when He had given thanks, He brake it and gave it to His disciples, saying, Take eat; this is My body, which is given for you. This do in remembrance of Me. After the same manner also He took the cup when He had supped [eaten supper], and when He had given thanks, He gave it to them, saying, Drink ye all of it [all of you drink it]; this cup is the new testament [new covenant, agreement] in My blood, which is shed for you for the remission of sins. This do, as oft as ye drink it, in remembrance of Me."

The next day, Good Friday, our Savior was to give His body and blood in death as the sacrifice for all human sin. By His suffering and death and rising again He would win forgiveness of sins for us. He wanted to provide a means by which He would give and we would receive that which He had won for us. The forgiveness which He won for us over 1,900 years ago He gives us today through the Gospel ("For I am not ashamed of the Gospel of Christ; for it is the power of God unto salvation to every one that believeth," Rom. 1:16); through Holy Baptism ("He that believeth and is baptized shall be saved," Mark 16:16); and through the Holy Communion ("For this is My blood of the new testament, which is shed for many for the remission of sins," Matt. 26:28).

It is God who gives us our life. He gives us physical life and spiritual life. If God does not give us our life, both physical and spiritual, we cannot have it. God gives, and we receive. He alone can forgive sins. All things come from Him. No matter how old a person is, if he becomes a Christian at all, he becomes one by God's work alone. So long as the Christian lives he is in need of that which God alone can give. God gives us faith and keeps us in faith by the means of the forgiving Gospel and Sacraments. Faith cannot rise by itself. It feeds upon the forgiving Word of God. It lays hold of forgiveness. And where there is forgiveness of sins there is also life and salvation. However, if a person refuses to receive God's Word, he becomes spiritually sick and dies. The Christian is to be active in hearing the Word and going to the Sacrament, by faith accepting and receiving God's acts of grace.

In his Large Catechism Martin Luther speaks of the "food of the soul" which Christ gives the baptized Christian in the Sacrament of the Altar. He reminds us that our Lord Jesus Christ instituted this sacrament of His holy body and blood as a means through and in which we obtain the remission of sins.

In the prayers after the Communion, as a part of the service, we thank God that He has refreshed us through this salutary gift, that He has given us pardon and peace in this sacrament; and we ask Him that He would strengthen us through this sacrament in faith toward Him and in fervent love toward one another; that He would rule in our hearts and minds by His Holy Spirit that we may be enabled constantly to serve Him. Truly this is a most wonderful and rich blessing which Christ has given us to help us along the way of our Christian life.

There are people who ask: How can this be? How can Christ give us His body and blood, forgiveness of sins, strength to live under Him in His kingdom, and the enabling power to "love God and one another," as the prayer says?

It is true that in the Holy Communion our eyes see nothing but ordinary bread and wine. Our faith, however, trusting in the words of Christ, grasps what our Lord promises, namely, "This is My body given for you. . . . This is My blood shed for the remission of your sins."

Christ cannot tell us a lie. He says that when we receive the bread in this sacrament, we receive also His body, and when we receive the wine, we receive also His blood given and shed for the remission of sins. More, our Lord said, "given for *you*" and "shed for *you*." Luther says that these words "for you" require all hearts to believe.

This is a mystery we cannot understand with our minds, of course. We can only believe it because we trust our Lord Jesus Christ. His word is true and reliable. We eat and drink, believing that He gives us what He says He will give. Therefore, if we ask the question: What is the Sacrament of the Altar? we answer: "It is the true body and blood of our Lord Jesus Christ, under [along with] the bread and wine, for us Christians to eat and to drink, instituted by Christ Himself."

We should be careful to note here that the bread and wine in the Holy Communion do not simply *represent* the body and blood of Christ. Nor are the bread and wine *changed* into the body and blood of Christ. Nor yet are the bread and wine *united* with the body and blood of Christ in such fashion that there is a third substance in the sacrament different from both. The Bible does not tell us that anything like this happens. We believe that the bread and wine remain real bread and wine; but that when we receive them in the Holy Communion, there is a communion (a union of one thing with another) of the bread and wine with the body and blood of Christ. This union has been called "the sacramental union." It happens only in this sacrament.

When St. Paul wanted to explain to the Corinthians what happens in the Lord's Supper, wanting them to understand what they were doing when they ate and drank the bread and wine, he asked, "The cup of blessing which we bless [the cup of wine], is it not the communion of the blood of Christ? The bread which we break, is it not the communion of the body of Christ?" (1 Cor. 10:16). St. Paul again emphasizes what is received in the sacrament when he wrote to the Corinthians who were profaning the sacrament, making it a meal for mere eating and drinking, much like any other meal. He warns them with these stern words: "Whoever, therefore, eats the bread and drinks the cup of the Lord in an unworthy manner will be guilty of profaning the body and blood of the Lord" (1 Cor. 11:27 RSV). Note that St. Paul does not say that one will be guilty of profaning bread and wine, but that he who eats bread and drinks wine in the sacrament in an unworthy manner (not distinguishing it from common bread and wine and not believing it to be the holy body and blood of Christ) will be guilty of profaning the body and blood of Christ.

These passages by St. Paul tell us that when the communicant receives the bread, he also receives the body of Christ, and that when he receives the wine, he also receives the blood of Christ. Lutherans have always believed in the "real presence" of the body and blood of Christ in the sacrament, trusting the words of Christ, "This is My body; this is My blood."

Lutherans have not tried to explain these words to mean anything else than that with the bread and wine Christ gives us His body and blood. We eat the bread and drink the wine and believe that we receive together with it the body and blood of Christ given and shed for us for the remission of sins. Christ makes this possible by His almighty power.

The chart below will summarize in a brief way what is taught and believed about the Holy Communion in the various churches:

REFORMED	LUTHERAN	ROMAN CATHOLIC
Bread — B̶o̶d̶y	Bread — Body	B̶r̶e̶a̶d̶ — Body
Wine — B̶l̶o̶o̶d	Wine — Blood	W̶i̶n̶e̶ — Blood
(only bread and wine are present in the Sacrament and received)	(both bread and wine and body and blood are present in the Sacrament and are received by every communicant)	(only body and blood are present in the Sacrament and received)

II. It is proper that we should discuss now the manner in which the Christian partakes of the Sacrament of the Altar, or participates in the Holy Communion.

Forgiveness of sins, life, and salvation are offered to all who partake of the sacrament. However, these benefits or blessings are accepted and possessed by only those who believe the words of Christ, "Given and shed for you for the remission of sins." The impenitent and unbelieving, if they participate in the Holy Communion, receive the body and blood of Christ also, but they receive it in a way that brings them under God's judgment. They do not receive the sacrament in a worthy manner. This does not please God. This "visible" Word in the sacrament makes the same demands upon us and brings us under the same judgment as the "spoken" Word. We cannot despise God's Word, His offer of grace, without penalty.

St. Paul says that those who eat and drink in the Holy Communion are to "examine" themselves. They are to "make trial" of themselves. The Christian is to examine himself in his heart. The sacrament can only be grasped and received by faith. Such a gift cannot be seized with the hand or taken with the mouth alone. Fasting and prayer and the like may have their place so that one's body may behave properly and reverently toward the body and blood of Christ. But the body does not grasp the sacrament. This is done by the faith of the heart which discerns and desires this treasure. When one "discerns the body," which St. Paul in 1 Cor. 11:29 tells us we must do if we are not to eat and drink God's judgment upon ourselves, he in faith distinguishes the elements in the sacrament to be different from common food and believes that they are the means by which Christ gives us His body and blood and joins us to Himself and His death.

The Christian will examine himself before God. He will "inspect" himself spiritually. He will ask, "Do I truly repent of my sins? Do I stand before God confessing my sin and guilt, knowing that it offends Him and would bring

His wrath and judgment upon me if it were not for my Savior? Do I trust the power of Christ to forgive me? Do I, as Christ's own redeemed and forgiven one, have the good and earnest purpose with the aid of the Holy Spirit to do better, to seek and pray in faith for the strength in Christ to overcome sin and evil in my life?"

We come to the sacrament "truly worthy and well prepared" when we come with penitent and believing hearts. For what is repentance if not an earnest attack on the old man at the beginning of a new life? And what is believing if not the laying hold in faith of all that Christ has to give? We are never to come to receive the sacrament in the sense of deserving, but of earnestly desiring the benefits offered in the sacrament.

Our nature is to rely on ourselves. We may attempt to cover up our sins and hold on to them, thinking that maybe they aren't so bad. They are quite wrong. We must realize that in us there is only sin and death from which we can in no way set ourselves free. And we must trust solely and alone in the forgiving mercy of Christ. Our worthiness is not in anything that we are or in anything that we can do, but our worthiness before God is in what Christ gives us through faith. Actually, the blessing in the sacrament does not at all depend on any worthiness in ourselves. We come as poor, miserable people, precisely because we are unworthy. He is truly worthy and well prepared who trusts Christ alone, looking only to Him and His worthiness. This is what the writer of the hymn had in mind when he wrote:

> *Oh, grant that I in manner worthy*
> *May now approach Thy heavenly Board*
> *And, as I lowly bow before Thee,*
> *Look only unto Thee, O Lord.*
>
> *Lutheran Hymnal,* 315

Those who do not know what they seek in the Holy Communion or why they come are not to participate in it.

The words "as often as you do it" imply that we are to receive the sacrament often. These words are added to the words of institution because Christ wishes the sacrament to be free for the Christian to use in faith whenever and wherever he will, according to everyone's opportunity and need. The Christian is not bound by rules or regulations in this mattter.

However, the Christian is not granted the liberty to despise the sacrament, for if he does that, he might as well take the liberty not to be a Christian. People who do not receive the sacrament over a long period of time are not to be considered Christians, according to the Large Catechism, for Christ did not institute the sacrament to be used as a mere spectacle, but He gave it for Christians to eat and drink for the regular remission of their sins. Christians who are seriously in the fight against sin and are striving toward holiness of life will receive the sacrament frequently, again and again, believing that "where there is forgiveness of sins there is also life and salvation."

Our Lord instituted the sacrament because we need it. He impressed this fact on us when He twice said: "This do in remembrance of Me." We can believe that when He said this, He was saying: "When you eat and drink My body and blood, recall to mind and think about My life lived for you, but especially recall to mind and think about My death for you for the forgiveness of your sins. Remember *Me!* Remember again all about Me. Remember that for you I rose again from the dead and that for you I sit now at the right hand of God with all power. Remember that I intercede for you before the throne of God, pleading My sacrifice for the sins of all men. Remember that I lived a perfect life for you. Remember that I died for you. Remember that I rose again for you. Remember that I am coming again for you. Believe that your sins are forgiven, that you have life and salvation which I give you, and that you shall be in heaven with Me forever." The memory of what Christ has done for us at so great a price must always fill us with joy and thanksgiving as we come to the sacrament.

In this study of the Sacrament of the Altar we ought to note that, as in Holy Baptism, we have (1) the sign, (2) the significance, and (3) the faith. The *sign* in the Sacrament of the Altar is the visible bread and wine. This we receive with the mouth. We can taste it and feel it. The *significance* is the spiritual blessing and result, namely union with Christ and with one another in the communion of saints. The *faith* should bring the *sign* and *significance* together, that is, the eating and drinking gives us Christ, unites us with Him in faith and love; it also unites us with our fellow Christians in faith and love. The sacrament works the joining together of Christ and all believers through faith.

Our union with Christ enables us to be "all one bread and one body" in the fellowship we have with one another. That is why we confess "I believe in the communion of saints" (the fellowship of the holy people of God in Christ).

In his *Christian Questions with Their Answers,* Luther asks the question: Finally, why do you wish to go to the Sacrament? He answers: That I may learn to believe that Christ died for *my* sin out of great love, as before said; and that I may also learn of Him to love God and my neighbor.

It is truly proper that we thank God again and again for His grace to us. He calls us to life with Him, and sustains us in that life, because He loves us. And to make sure that the gift of love does not escape us He established His church, gave the Word and the Sacraments, and through the work of the Holy Spirit continues ceaselessly to hold the gift before us.

To treat the Sacrament of the Altar lightly is to doubt or despise the generosity of God's love. To receive it frequently and to thank Him for it is the precious privilege of all His believing children.

And now a final word at the close of our *Studies in Lutheran Doctrine.* Always remember that you have been bought with a price. Christ Jesus has died for your sins. He has paid the full price. Through the work of the Holy Spirit you are a child of God. Therefore:

> *"Sanctify in your heart Christ
> as Lord, and be ready always
> to give an answer to every
> man who asks you a reason
> for the hope that is in you."*
> *(1 Peter 3:15)*

The following exercises are meant to help you. You will discover that it is much easier to begin reading the text with your exercise beside you and to answer the questions as you read. Looking at the question and then trying to find the answer will take more time than if you follow the suggestion we make. If you work from your exercise and just try to find answers, you will get confused, miss the meaning of the text, and waste your time.

Please do not turn in any exercise unless *every question* is answered. Your pastor will first check to see that you have left no questions unanswered. Should he find any he will return the exercise to you with an *incomplete*.

Remember also that you are preparing for examinations which will be given later. It will be good if you use your talents to do the best you can, and that in all things you be faithful. May God bless you as you learn more about the treasure which is yours.

Lesson No. 1 *("Who Am I?")* Name or Code Number _____

A. Read as much as is necessary to answer the questions in this lesson.

B. Do memory work as assigned by the pastor.

C. Come prepared to discuss: (1) Why is Bible study important to us? List as many reasons as you can, and bring the list to class. (2) What are some of the important things we would not know if we did not have the Bible? List them, and bring them to class.

The Exercise:

1. One question men have always wondered about is _____

_____

2. The *organic view* of man says that _____

_____

_____

3. How is man different from other creatures? _____

_____

4. What will happen to man if he is left to himself? How will he grow and develop? What will he be

like if he is not changed through the power of God? _____

_____

_____

5. Which problem is older than man? _____

6. What is a *point of reference?* _____

_____

7. What are some things we could not know about if we did not have the Bible? _____

_____

_____

8. God gave man the *freedom of his will.* What does this mean? What happened to this freedom when

man turned against God? _____

_____

_____

Lesson No. 2 *("Who Am I?")*   Name or Code Number _____

    A. Finish reading the chapter on the nature of man, "Who Am I?"

    B. Do memory work as assigned by the pastor.

    C. Come prepared to discuss: (1) Do you think that man can ever put God's creation together again so it will be like it was in the beginning? Why or why not?

The Exercise:

1. What are some of the things man began to wonder about before he turned against God? _____

_____

_____

2. When Satan tempted man to sin, what was the question he asked? _____

_____

3. Why didn't God want Adam and Eve to eat the fruit of the tree? _____

_____

4. What did Satan say the reason was for God telling Adam and Eve not to eat the fruit of the tree? ___

_____

_____

5. What was the relationship between God and man before man disobeyed God? _____

_____

6. Why were Adam and Eve so afraid after they had sinned? _____

7. Read Genesis 1:27, 28. What three things did God tell man to do to the earth, and all living things

on it? _____

_____

8. What is *original sin?* _____

_____

9. Read Romans 5:12. Why must all men die? _____

_____

10. Read John 3:3-5. If man is to be restored to the kingdom of heaven, what must happen to him? ___

_____

Lesson No. 3 *("What Do I Believe?")*   Name or Code Number _____

A. Read as much as is necessary to answer the questions in this lesson.

B. Do memory work as assigned by the pastor.

C. Come prepared to discuss: (1) If all of the people in these United States were atheists, what would our country probably be like? (2) Make believe that you are an atheist and want to prove that there is no God. What would you have to say while trying to prove this?

The Exercise:

1. What are the three different kinds of people in the world? _____

_____

_____

2. What is an "atheist"? _____

3. What does the word "atheos" mean? _____

4. What has Russian Communism failed to do? _____

Why? _____

5. What do most atheists have to say about religion? _____

_____

6. What is the first question an atheist will usually ask? _____

_____

7. Which question can the believer ask the atheist? _____

_____

8. What are some of the things an atheist must wonder about? _____

_____

9. While the believer says that God created everything, the atheist says that _____

_____

10. Is it hard for you to believe that the world just "happened by chance"? _____ Why or

why not? _____

_____

153

Lesson No. 4 *("What Do I Believe?")*   Name or Code Number _____

A. Read as much as is necessary to answer the questions in this lesson.

B. Do memory work as assigned by the pastor.

C. Come prepared to discuss: (1) List at least ten things that you do every day in which you show that you have faith and trust in something or someone. Example: "Each day I turn on the water faucet and believe that water will come out." (2) List at least five ways in which you show that you have faith in God.

The Exercise:

1. A true agnostic is a person who _____

_____

2. A person cannot grow up to be a thoughtful and honest Christian unless _____

_____

3. What must one do in order to grow emotionally, mentally, and spiritually? _____

_____

_____

4. When you have doubts, what should you do about them? _____

_____

What should you not do about them? _____

_____

5. If you hear someone say, "God did not get things started," you can be sure that this is not a scientific

statement. Why? _____

_____

6. What is the difference between a "true" agnostic, and a "false" agnostic? _____

_____

_____

7. What does the "pantheist" believe about God? _____

_____

8. Why doesn't pantheism offer us any hope? _____

_____ (turn page over)

Lesson No. 4 continued

9. What does the deist believe about God? _____

_____

_____

10. Why isn't a deist a Christian? _____

_____

_____

_____

11. The Apostles' Creed is a theistic creed. How do we know this? _____

_____

_____

12. The Apostles' Creed is also a _____ creed. What does this mean? _____

_____

_____

_____

13. Why is the teaching (doctrine) of the Trinity known as the "great mystery"? _____

_____

_____

_____

14. The "doctrine" of the Trinity is often called "the great Three in One." Who are the three in one? ___

_____

15. A "creed" is a statement about what? _____

_____

Lesson No. 5 *("What Do I Believe?")*   Name or Code Number _____

A. Read as much as is necessary to answer the questions in this lesson.

B. Do memory work as assigned by the pastor.

C. Come prepared to discuss: (1) Do you think it would be good for people from different nations and religions to get together and talk about their belief in God? Why or why not? (2) What do you think about people who say, "It doesn't make any difference what you believe about God as long as you believe it sincerely"?

The Exercise:

1. What is the difference between what a Moslem and a Christian will say about God? _____
_____
_____

2. Christians believe that they can say some things about God because _____
_____

3. List at least two Scripture passages which tell us that when we see and believe in Jesus we are also seeing and believing in God. _____
_____

4. What is one thing we must do if we want to learn about God? _____
_____

5. "God is eternal." What does this mean? _____
_____

6. "God is unchangeable." What does this mean? _____
_____

7. "God is omnipotent." What does this mean? _____

8. We say that God knows all things. What do we call this attribute? God is _____
_____

9. "God is omnipresent." What does this mean? _____
_____

10. Why is it difficult for us to imagine that God is holy? _____
_____

Lesson No. 6 *("What Do I Believe?")*   Name or Code Number _____

A. Read as much as is necessary to answer the questions in this lesson.

B. Do memory work as assigned by the pastor.

C. In place of the discussion questions for today the pastor will give a lecture on Martin Luther's struggle with the "righteousness of God."

The Exercise:

1. God is righteous in two important ways. What are they? _____
_____

2. In 2 Timothy 2:13 what does St. Paul say about God? _____
_____ What does this mean?_____
_____

3. What does it mean when we say that the Lord is gracious? _____
_____

4. "God is Love." Where do we get this picture of God? _____

5. What is the difference between "infatuation" and the love of God? _____
_____

_____

6. What is the difference between the love God has for man and the love people have for each other? ___
_____

_____

_____

7. Love is more than a "power." Love is a _____ and that _____ is _____.

8. Why do we love God? _____
_____

_____

9. When we see Jesus we know that God is _____.

10. When Jesus says, "Your sins are forgiven," we know that _____
_____

_____

Lesson No. 7 *("Who Is God?")*   Name or Code Number _____

The First Article

   A. Read as much as is necessary to answer the questions in this lesson.

   B. Do memory work as assigned by the pastor.

   C. Come prepared to discuss: (1) What are some things which a person must believe before he or she can be a good citizen of this country? (2) What are some things which a person must believe in when he or she is a citizen of the kingdom of God?

The Exercise:

1. Which personal pronoun gives a creed its meaningfulness? _____

2. God is not dead just because _____

3. We could say that the word "believe" means _____

4. When St. Paul speaks about the heart, he may be thinking of it as being _____

   _____

5. When Jesus said, "By their fruits you shall know them," what was He talking about? _____

   _____

   _____

6. If a confession is sincere and true, what should follow? _____

   _____

7. When one says, "I believe in God," what is the deepest meaning of this statement? _____

   _____

8. The power to believe is a gift. What is this gift called? _____

   _____

9. Why should a Christian be able to rest secure in God's loving care, and also do acts of faith? _____

   _____

   _____

   _____

10. How do we know that God is the Maker of heaven and earth? _____

   _____

11. God holds all the power of the universe within Himself. By this we mean that He is _____

Lesson No. 8 *("Who Is God?")*   Name or Code Number _____

The First Article

A. Read as much as is necessary to answer the questions in this lesson.

B. Do memory work as assigned by the pastor.

C. Come prepared to discuss: (1) From the catechism answer the question, "Why is it important to know about God?" (2) From the first ten chapters in the Book of Acts show that people who believe in God are willing to suffer for their faith in Christ.

The Exercise:

1. Of all the gifts of God mentioned in the First Article, which do you think is the most important? ____

_____ Why? _____

_____

_____

2. God has not only given us life, but He has also given us _____

_____

3. Read Matthew 25:14-30. What does this parable teach? _____

_____

4. Of all the gifts of God, which should be most important to all people? _____

_____

_____

5. Write at least a 150-word essay on what God has given you. (Use a separate sheet of paper.)

Lesson No. 9 *("Who Is God?")*   Name or Code Number _____

The Second Article

    A. Read as much as is necessary to answer the questions in this lesson.

    B. Do memory work as assigned by the pastor.

    C. Come prepared to discuss: Do you think that a person who says the following things is a Christian? Why or why not? "I believe in God. My God created all things. My God created me, and my God is almighty. My God is in all things, and in every human being."

The Exercise:

1. Not everyone who says he believes in God is a _____.

2. One of the first things we mean when we say, "I believe in Jesus," is _____
_____

3. Explain two ways in which the name "Christ" can be used. _____
_____

4. What are the two meanings of the statement that "Jesus is the Son of God"?

    (a) _____ _____

    (b) _____

5. What is meant in John 1:14, "The Word was made flesh and dwelt among us"? _____
_____
_____

6. What do we mean when we say that Jesus was true man? _____
_____
_____

7. When are people called "sons of God"? _____
_____

8. Explain the ways in which we are not like the people God has meant us to be. _____
_____
_____

Lesson No. 10 *("Who Is God?")*   Name or Code Number _____

The Second Article

   A. Read as much as is necessary to answer the questions in this lesson.

   B. Do memory work as assigned by the pastor.

   C. Come prepared to discuss: Read the 53d chapter of Isaiah and come prepared to discuss why Christians believe that this chapter is a prophecy of Christ's life.

The Exercise:

1. Who was the Roman governor of Judea under whom Jesus suffered? _____
_____

2. On which day did Jesus die? _____

3. Which Old Testament writer prophesied that not a bone in Jesus' body would be broken? _____
_____

4. What did the disciples say when they were told to stop saying that Jesus had risen from the dead? ____
_____
_____

5. The great message of Easter is that "because He lives, we, too, _____
_____

6. In John 14:1-3 Jesus gives us a promise. What is that promise? _____
_____

7. Why could the followers of Jesus be so sure that He was risen from the dead? _____
_____

8. How is Jesus still present with us today? _____
_____

9. Jesus ascended into heaven. What does this mean? _____
_____
_____

10. What happens when two or three people are gathered together in the name of Jesus? _____
_____

Lesson No. 11 *("Who Is God?")* Name or Code Number _____

The Second Article

A. Read as much as is necessary to answer the questions in this lesson.

B. Do memory work as assigned by the pastor.

C. Come prepared to discuss the theory of reincarnation. Prepare to do this by going to your encyclopedia or some other reference book to find the meaning of this theory. Then discover if this is a Christian view, and why or why not.

The Exercise:

1. Jesus sits at the right hand of God. What does this mean? _____
_____

2. When will Jesus come again to this earth? _____
_____

3. What happens to people who cannot see or say that they are sinners? _____
_____

4. How do we know that Jesus will come again? _____
_____

5. If you say that Jesus is your Lord, what does this mean? _____
_____

6. What promise are you repeating when you take your confirmation vows? _____
_____

7. Why don't most people want Jesus to be their Lord? _____
_____

8. On another sheet of paper, write in 100 words or more why you think most people are afraid to let Jesus be the Lord of their lives. _____
_____

Lesson No. 12 *("Who Is God?")*   Name or Code Number _____

The Second Article

    A. Finish reading this chapter on the Second Article.

    B. Do memory work as assigned by the pastor.

    C. Come prepared to discuss:

        There are some people who believe that man can and will build a world in which there is little or no crime and war. What do you think about this? Do you think it can be done? Why, or why not?

The Exercise:

1. What is the meaning of the word "redeem"? _____

2. What are some things we mean when we say that man is "lost"? _____

_____

_____

_____

3. We have been condemned to death because of our _____

4. What wonderful news does St. Paul give us in Romans 5:8? _____

_____

_____

5. John 3:16 is one of the most well-known verses in the Bible. What does it say? _____

_____

_____

_____

6. Jesus became "sin" for us. What does this mean?_____

_____

_____

7. We can really and truly believe that we shall rise from the dead because _____

_____

8. Using Luther's words, tell how Jesus purchased and won us from sin and death, and the power of the

    devil? _____

_____

_____

(turn page over)

9. Jesus is your "Substitute." What does this mean? _____

_____

_____

10. Why are you no longer a stranger to God? _____

_____

_____

11. Using Luther's words, tell why we have been saved. _____

_____

12. How can you thank and praise God for His love? (This must be your own answer. List as many ways
    as you can.)

_____

_____

_____

_____

_____

_____

_____

_____

_____

_____

_____

_____

_____

_____

_____

_____

Lesson No. 13 *("Who Is God?")*   Name or Code Number _____

The Third Article

    A. Read as much as is necessary to answer the questions in this lesson.

    B. Do memory work as assigned by the pastor.

    C. Come prepared to discuss:

        What do you think the most important things are for people who want to become mature? What must they do? What kind of discipline must one put upon himself if he is to become mature? What are some of the things which keep people from growing up to be mature adults?

The Exercise:

1. Name and describe (as best you can) the four kinds of growth for human beings. _____

_____

_____

_____

_____

2. The five main points of the Third Article are _____

_____

_____

_____

3. What did Jesus say that the Holy Spirit would do for His disciples? _____

_____

_____

4. Luther says that the first thing which the Holy Ghost does is _____

_____

5. In the Christian religion we get a picture of God which is not found in other religions. What is this

   picture? _____

_____

6. "The Holy Ghost enlightens me with His gifts." What does this mean? Write at least 100 words on this

   subject on another sheet of paper.

174

Lesson No. 14 *("Who Is God?")*   Name or Code Number _____

The Third Article

    A. Read as much as is necessary to answer the questions in this lesson.

    B. Do memory work as assigned by the pastor.

    C. Come prepared to discuss:

       If we want to be disciples of Jesus Christ, what are some of the things which we must decide to do?

The Exercise:

1. The Holy Ghost has "sanctified me in the true faith." What does this mean? _____
_____

2. When we are in the process of being sanctified, we are becoming new kinds of people. Which Scripture

    passage would lead us to believe this? _____
_____

3. Who gives us the power to grow to greater Christian maturity? _____
_____

4. What is the "process" of sanctification? _____

    How long does it take? _____
_____

5. The Christian religion has no place within it for man to say, _____
_____

6. Faith in Jesus Christ comes from God as a _____

7. What is at least one difference between Christianity and other religions? _____
_____

8. Why are all people "on the same level" in the eyes of God? _____
_____
_____

9. Sanctification is the process of _____

10. The Holy Spirit gives us new _____ and makes _____
_____

The Third Article

(At least two weeks needed)

    A. Do the necessary amount of reading.

    B. Do memory work as assigned by the pastor.

    C. Answer at least one half of the questions in this exercise.

    D. Because of the material, no special discussion questions are given. A pastor's discussion of the congregation's organizational structure is suggested.

The Exercise:

1. In order to understand the meaning of "the church," we must go back to _____

_____

2. What did Jesus say to Peter in Matthew 16:18? _____

_____

What does the Roman (Catholic) Church say these words mean? _____

_____

What does the Lutheran Church (most of it) believe that these words mean? _____

_____

_____

3. We do know that where there is no faith in Jesus Christ as the Son of God, there is no _____

_____

4. List some of the things which people do when they form a congregation. _____

_____

_____

_____

5. What did Martin Luther say that the holy Christian Church is? _____

_____

_____

6. The holy Christian Church has been _____ , _____

_____ , _____ by the Holy Ghost, and is daily increased by the means of

the _____ , and _____ . (turn page over)

Lessons No. 15 and 16 continued

7. When Luther said that the church is "visible," what was he talking about? What is visible about the church, or what can we see to know that the church is present? _____

_____

_____

_____

8. Where Jesus is in the midst of two or three people, there also is the _____

_____

9. The church is given life by the _____

10. We also must remember that we cannot live as Christians without _____

_____

11. There is no such thing as an _____ Christian. What does this mean? _____

_____

_____

12. Why did St. Paul want to go to Rome according to his words in Romans 1:11, 12? _____

_____

_____

13. The church rests securely on the foundation of _____

_____

14. Thinking of the church, what did Jesus mean in John 15:4-5? _____

_____

_____

15. Read Ephesians 2:19-22. What are we to be in the church? _____

_____

16. Belonging to the church is belonging to _____

17. What did Jesus mean when He said that the "gates of hell" shall not prevail against the church? _____

_____

_____

18. If nothing can separate us from the love of God which is in Christ Jesus our Lord, then we, the believers in Christ shall _____

19. Who or what is the church of Jesus Christ? _____

20. The church is made up of all _____

_____

21. What does St. Paul ask us to do in Ephesians 4:1-6? _____

_____

_____

Lesson No. 17 ("*Who Is God?*") Name or Code Number _____

The Third Article

A. Read as much as is necessary to answer the questions in this lesson.

B. Do memory work as assigned by the pastor.

C. It is suggested that the pastor might want to conduct a discussion on the congregation's organization.

The Exercise:

1. Why is the church called *holy?* _____

_____

_____

2. What is the *Communion of Saints?* _____

_____

3. How are the people of God united to God? _____

_____

4. What is *original sin?* _____

_____

5. When the Church talks about the *new man* and the *old man* what does this mean? How does a Christian become a new man every day? _____

_____

_____

_____

_____

6. How does God bring the forgiveness of sins to us? _____

_____

7. What do the Scriptures tell us is going to happen on the *Last Day?* _____

_____

8. Why isn't the Christian afraid of the Day of Judgment? _____

_____

_____

9. Why are Christians so sure of a life everlasting? _____

_____

10. Who is the "resurrection and the life"? _____

_____

Lesson No. 18 *("How Should I Live?")*   Name or Code Number _____

The First Commandment

   A. Read as much as is necessary to answer the questions in this lesson.

   B. Do memory work as assigned by the pastor.

   C. Read Matthew 22:36-38; Exodus, 32.

   D. Bring new clippings that demonstrate the breaking of this commandment.

The Exercise:

1. List at least five *false gods* which people can worship and do worship. _____

   _____

   _____

2. Read Luke 12:16-21 and tell what this man's greatest mistake was. _____

   _____

3. What is a *false god?* _____

   _____

4. Why should we be thankful that God has let us know what He wants of us? _____

   _____

5. On another sheet of paper write (in 100 words or more) how people break the First Commandment

   at home, at school, at play, and in church.

Lesson No. 19 *("How Should I Live?")*   Name or Code Number _____

The Second Commandment

    A. Read the material on the Second Commandment.

    B. Do memory work as assigned by the pastor.

    C. Read Exodus 20:7; Lev. 19:12; Gal. 6:7.

The Exercise:

1. How is the name of the Lord to be used? _____

_____

2. St. Paul says, "Be not deceived; God is not mocked." What does this mean in the Second Command-

ment? _____

_____

_____

3. What is perjury, and why is it so serious? _____

_____

_____

4. Why do you think people take the name of the Lord in vain? _____

_____

_____

5. Write on another sheet of paper at least 100 words on ways in which Christians can keep this command-

ment at home, at school, at play, and at church.

Lesson No. 20 *("How Should I Live?")*　　　　　Name or Code Number _____

The Third Commandment

 A. Read the material on the Third Commandment.

 B. Do memory work as assigned by the pastor. It is suggested that the pastor discuss the church year at this point.

 C. Read: Genesis 2:2, 3; Isaiah 58:13, 14; Mark 2:27, 28.

The Exercise:

1. How did Christians decide to meet on Sundays for regular worship? _____

_____

2. What is the most important reason for people to go to church regularly? _____

_____

_____

3. List some good excuses for staying away from church. _____

_____

_____

4. What do you think Jesus means to tell us in Mark 2:27? _____

_____

 Mark 2:28? _____

_____

5. In 100 words or more (on another sheet of paper) write what you think about Christians keeping their place of business open on Sunday. Should they or shouldn't they? When is it necessary or not necessary? Is it necessary at all? Do you think business on Sunday should be against the law? Explain all you say.

Lesson No. 21 *("How Should I Live?")*   Name or Code Number _____

The Fourth Commandment

    A. Read the material on the Fourth Commandment.

    B. Do memory work as assigned by the pastor.

    C. Read Genesis 47:1-12; Ephesians 6:2, 3; Romans 13:1-7.

    D. Come prepared to discuss the things children have a right to expect from their parents and the things parents have a right to expect from their children.

The Exercise:

1. Do you think teen-agers should be treated as a separate group of people? Why or why not? _____

_____

_____

_____

2. Do you agree with Luther's explanation to the Fourth Commandment? Why? _____

_____

_____

3. What do you think it means to honor your parents and masters? _____

_____

4. Write at least 250 words on the subject. . . . "What I Think Is Necessary for People to Do in Order to Live Happily Together As a Family." Include the responsibilities which people must accept for themselves and others. Do this on another sheet of paper.

Lesson No. 22 *("How Should I Live?")* Name or Code Number _____

The Fifth Commandment

    A. Read the material on the Fifth Commandment.

    B. Do memory work as assigned by the pastor.

    C. Read Genesis 9:6; Matthew 5:5, 7, 9; Matthew 26:52; Romans 12:19, 20; Ephesians 4:32; 1 John 3:15.

The Exercise:

1. What does 1 John 3:15 say about hatred? _____

_____

2. Write in 100 words or more what you think about capital punishment? Is it right or wrong? Is it sometimes right and sometimes wrong? Can a Christian act as an executioner of a man who has killed and been sentenced to death? Give reasons. (Use another sheet of paper.)

3. Write in 100 words or more what you think about Christians going to war and killing other people. What would you do if you were asked to drop an atom bomb on a city and kill hundreds and thousands of people? Give your reasons. (Use another sheet of paper.)

Lesson No. 23 *("How Should I Live?")*   Name or Code Number _____

The Sixth Commandment

    A. Read the material on the Sixth Commandment.

    B. Do memory work as assigned by the pastor.

    C. Read Genesis 2:18-24; Matthew 5:27, 28; Matthew 19:6; 1 Corinthians 6:19, Ephesians 5:3, 4; Philipians 4:8.

The Exercise:

1. In 100 words or more tell what you think about laws against selling certain kinds of magazines with stories and pictures in them which are filthy.

2. Write in 100 words or more how you can best prepare yourself for a happy marriage.

The Seventh Commandment

    A. Read the material on the Seventh Commandment.

    B. Do memory work as assigned by the pastor.

    C. Come prepared to discuss: (1) What do you think would happen in a city if stealing were made legal? (2) What do you think is the solution to cheating in our schools? (3) How do many young persons steal from their community and their God when they are in school?

The Exercise:

1. What is one possible reason why God gave the Seventh Commandment? _____

_____

2. What are the two parts of this commandment? _____

_____

_____

3. What is stealing? _____

_____

4. List at least five kinds of stealing which are well accepted by many people today. _____

_____

_____

_____

5. What must one do for his neighbor in order to keep this commandment? _____

_____

6. What is the worst kind of stealing? _____

_____

7. How many things can you list that belong to you? _____

_____

8. What three main gifts has God given you to use? _____

_____

9. What is the main teaching in Matthew 25:14-30? _____

Lesson No. 25 ("How Should I Live?")   Name or Code Number _____

The Eighth Commandment

    A. Read the chapter on the Eighth Commandment and Psalm 50:19-22; Proverbs 19:5; Matthew 18:15; Matthew 25:59-61; Luke 6:37.

    B. Do memory work as assigned by the pastor.

    C. Come prepared to discuss: (1) How do you think the evil of gossip can be eliminated from the Christian community (church)? (2) What are some of the things which happen to people who gossip? (3) What do you think of Jesus' words in Matthew 18:15? Are they easy or difficult to apply? Why?

The Exercise:

1. According to Jesus, who is your neighbor? _____

2. What is your Christian responsibility toward your neighbor? _____

_____

3. Most gossipers are _____

4. Why can't the Christian Church allow gossip? _____

_____

5. When a Christian is attacked, what doesn't he do? _____

_____

6. If you are guilty of the sin described in this commandment, what must you do? Why? ____

_____

_____

7. Why are lies and slanders against other people so serious? _____

_____

8. When is silence also a sin? _____

_____

_____

9. What does John 15:12 tell us to do? _____

_____

_____

10. What do you think John 15:12 means? _____

_____

_____

Ninth and Tenth Commandments

A. Read material on the Ninth and Tenth Commandments and 1 Timothy 6:8-10; Galatians 5:13.

B. Do memory work as assigned by the pastor.

C. Come to class prepared to discuss: (1) What do you think of the actions of some citizens of the United States when they display their wealth to less fortunate peoples of the earth, and boast, "We have more things than anyone else"? (2) Why (do you suppose) has the "having of things" come to be so important to us Americans?

The Exercise:

1. Define "covetousness" (see dictionary). ——————————————————————

——

2. Define "envy" (see dictionary). ————————————————————————

——

——

3. How are the Ninth and Tenth Commandments related to Commandment Eight? ——————

——

——

——

4. How do many people measure their success? ——————————————————

——

5. What did the sin of covetousness do to David? ——————————————————

——

6. What can happen when nations covet what other nations have? ——————————————

——

7. What do Christians have that money cannot buy? ————————————————————

——

8. What will the Christian do when his neighbor gets something which he does not have? ——————

——

9. Why doesn't the Christian have time to be covetous? ——————————————————

The Conclusion to the Ten Commandments

  A. Read the final chapter on the Ten Commandments and Galatians 3:10; Romans 6:23; Ezekiel 18:20; Luke 19:43, 44; 1 Timothy 4:8; Genesis 32:10; 1 John 5:3.

  B. Do memory work as assigned by the pastor.

  C. Come prepared to discuss: (1) What do you think God means when He says, "I am a jealous God"? (2) Do you think that God's threats are too hard or harsh? Explain. (3) What do you think would happen to God and His kingdom if He overlooked the sins of men? Explain.

The Exercise:

1. God is "merciful." What does this mean? _____

_____

2. Why should the "evil" person fear the commandments of God? _____

_____

3. Why can't the Christian claim to be ignorant of what God wants from him? _____ .

_____

4. Who is responsible for your conduct? Why? _____

_____

5. If you choose to do evil, whom can't you blame? _____

  Why? _____

6. If you do good, to whom do you owe thanks? _____ Why? _____

_____

7. What do some people say about their personal responsibility for sin? _____

_____ What do you think about this? _____

8. How can a person be forgiven for the sins he or she commits? _____

_____

Lesson No. 28 *("How Should I Pray?")*   Name or Code Number _____

The Lord's Prayer

    A. Read as much as is necessary to complete this lesson.

    B. Do memory work as assigned by the pastor.

    C. Discussion on the meaning and purpose of prayer. To be led by the pastor.

    D. Complete the exercise.

The Exercise:

  1. Why did Jesus teach His disciples how to pray? _____

  2. Into how many parts did Luther divide the Lord's Prayer? _____

  3. Why does God want us to pray "Our Father"? _____

_____

  4. Read Luke 15:11-32 and tell what you think Jesus wants us to learn from this story. _____

_____

  5. The "Our Father" does not only belong to you alone, but it also belongs to _____

  6. What is the First Petition of the Lord's Prayer? _____

  7. According to Luther, how is the name of God kept holy? _____

_____

  8. What is the Second Petition of the Lord's Prayer? _____

  9. You are in God's kingdom because _____

10. God's kingdom has the power and love to make _____

_____

11. When the kingdom comes, you start to be _____ from _____

     people in whom the kingdom is not. _____

12. The kingdom of God will move on to a final _____

(turn page over)

Lesson No. 28 continued

13. You are asking more than "May Thy kingdom come in me." What else are you asking for in this petition? _____

_____

_____

And what else will you do besides praying? _____

_____

14. What does Philippians 2:10 say will happen? _____

_____

15. What is the Third Petition? _____

_____

16. What are you inviting your heavenly Father to do with you when you pray this petition? _____

_____

17. Why is the will of God done perfectly in heaven? _____

_____

18. If you pray, "Thy will be done in me," what does this do to your right to choose for yourself? _____

_____

19. What is the one thing Christians know for sure about the will of God? _____

_____

Lesson No. 29 *("How Should I Pray?")*   Name or Code Number _____

The Lord's Prayer

    A. Finish reading the material on the Lord's Prayer.

    B. Review memory work, or do new memory work as may be assigned by the pastor.

The Exercise:

1. What is the Fourth Petition of the Lord's Prayer? _____

    _____

2. One purpose of this petition may be to help you _____

    _____, and _____

3. Why should one always say table prayers? _____

    _____

4. In the Fourth Petition you do not ask for more _____,

    nor are you asking for _____

5. In Matthew 6:25 Jesus asks the question _____

    _____

6. What does Jesus want to teach us in Matthew 6:28-33? _____

    _____

7. Man must earn his daily bread, but this he can do only because _____

    _____

8. What is the Fifth Petition? _____

    _____

9. Why do we say that there probably is nothing more direct and powerful in the Lord's Prayer than this

    petition? _____

    _____

    _____

10. What is the meaning of Matthew 7:2? _____

    _____ (turn page over)

Lesson No. 29 continued

11. How often did Jesus tell Simon Peter to forgive others? _____

_____

12. What was the prayer Jesus prayed on the cross which shows us how much He meant the words of this

petition? _____

_____

13. What does God say about our sins in Isaiah 43:25? _____

_____

14. Our sins put Jesus on the cross, but we are _____

15. What is the Sixth Petition? _____

16. What does this mean? _____

_____

_____

17. What is the Seventh Petition? _____

18. What does this mean? _____

_____

_____

19. The prayer of this petition is not to deliver you from suffering, but you pray to be delivered from

_____

20. What was evil about Jesus' suffering? _____

_____ What was good about it? _____

_____

21. In the remaining space, and in your own words, tell what the Conclusion to the Lord's Prayer means.

_____

_____

_____

_____

Lesson No. 30 *(The Office of the Keys and Confession)*   Name or Code Number _____

   A. Read the chapter on the Office of the Keys.

   B. Do memory work as assigned by the pastor.

The Exercise:

1. What is the Office of the Keys? _____

   _____

   _____

2. What is the function of this office? _____

   _____

   _____

3. Who has the power of the Keys? _____

   _____

4. What is the mark of a Christian and the members of the church? _____

   _____

5. How is the church to bring men, women, and children into the kingdom of God? _____

   _____

6. What must the church do when one of its members lives in open sin and refuses to repent? _____

   _____

   _____

   _____

7. What are the two parts of Confession? _____

   _____

8. List three kinds of confession. _____

   _____

9. What is the society of the concerned? _____

   _____

(turn page over)

10. When do you think it would be necessary and good for you to go and confess your sins to the pastor?

_____

_____

11. Why do you think so many people do not want to confess their sins to the pastor? _____

_____

12. Do you suppose that most people do not want other people to know how sinful they really are?

_____

Lessons No. 31 and 32 *(Holy Baptism)*   Name or Code Number _____

    A. Read the chapter on Holy Baptism.

    B. Do memory work as assigned by the pastor.

The Exercise:

1. What do we become when we are baptized? _____

_____

2. What is Christian Baptism? _____

_____

_____

3. What makes Holy Baptism more than just a handful of water? _____

_____

4. Who has commanded us to baptize? _____

5. What are the gifts and blessings of Holy Baptism? _____

6. How must we come into the kingdom of God? _____

_____

7. What is the sign in our baptism? _____

_____

8. What do we mean when we say that Holy Baptsm is a lifelong process? _____

_____

_____

9. What does Baptism signify according to Dr. Martin Luther? _____

_____

What does this mean? _____

_____

10. Explain why Baptism is more than giving a child a name. _____

_____

_____

(turn page over)

Lessons No. 31 and 32 continued

11. How long do the gifts and blessings of Baptism **last?** _____

_____

_____

12. What do we pray God to do for us? _____

_____

13. Where is the Word of God to touch our life again and again? _____

_____

Lessons No. 33 and 34 *(The Sacrament of the Altar)*   Name or Code Number _____

A. Read the chapter on the Sacrament of the Altar.

B. Do memory work as assigned by the pastor.

The Exercise:

1. Why is the Sacrament of the Altar also called the Lord's Supper? _____
_____

2. The Sacrament is also a communion. What does this mean? _____
_____
_____

3. Why did Jesus give us the Lord's Supper? _____
_____

4. How does God give us faith? _____
_____

5. Why must the baptized Christian receive the Lord's Supper often? _____
_____

6. What do we receive in the Lord's Supper? _____
_____

7. For whom has the blood of Christ been shed? _____
_____

8. For whom has the body of Christ been given? _____
_____

9. What do we mean when we say that the Sacrament is a mystery? _____
_____
_____

10. What does St. Paul say about those who take the Sacrament like mere eating and drinking? _____
_____
_____ (turn page over)

11. Lutherans believe in the real presence of Christ's body and blood in the Sacrament. What does this mean? _____

_____

12. What do the Roman Catholics believe about the Sacrament? _____

_____

_____

13. What do the Reformed Churches believe they receive in the Sacrament? _____

_____

14. What do Lutherans believe they receive in the Sacrament? _____

_____

15. Who is truly worthy and well prepared to take the Sacrament? _____

_____

_____

16. How often should a Christian go to the Lord's Supper? _____

_____ Why? _____

_____

17. What should we remember when we go to the Lord's Supper? _____

_____

_____

18. What is the sign in the Sacrament? _____

_____

19. What is the significance of the Sacrament? _____

_____

_____